AUTOEXEC.BAT Modifications

SET PATH = *<old path>*;\CLIPPER5\BIN;\CLIPPER5\NG

SET CLIPPER = [*<memory/file handle options>*]	Default memory specifications
SET CLIPPERCMD = [*<compiler option list>*]	Default compiler options
SET INCLUDE = *<path>*	Default include file location
SET LIB = *<path>*	Default library file location
SET OBJ = *<path>*	Default object file location
SET PLL = *<path>*	Default pre-link library file location
SET RMAKE = [*<option list>*]	Default make options
SET RTLINKCMD = [*<link option list>*]	Default link options
SET TMP = *<path>*	Default temporary file location

CLIPPER VARIABLES

Kind	*Lifetime*	*Visibility*	*Default Value*
Static	Permanent	Declaring procedure only	NIL
Local	Until end of declaring procedure	Declaring procedure	NIL
Private	Until end of declaring procedure	Declaring procedure and any procedures called	NIL
Public	Permanent	Entire program	.F.

The Up & Running Series from SYBEX

Other titles include Up & Running with:

- **AutoSketch 3**
- **Carbon Copy Plus**
- **DOS 3.3**
- **DOS 5**
- **DR DOS 5.0**
- **Flight Simulator**
- **Grammatik IV 2.0**
- **Harvard Graphics**
- **Lotus 1-2-3 Release 2.2**
- **Lotus 1-2-3 Release 2.3**
- **Lotus 1-2-3 Release 3.1**
- **Norton Utilities**
- **Norton Utilities 5**
- **Norton Utilities on the Macintosh**
- **PageMaker 4 on the PC**
- **PageMaker on the Macintosh**
- **PC Tools Deluxe 6**
- **PC-Write**
- **PROCOMM PLUS**
- **Q&A**
- **Q&A 4**
- **Quattro Pro 3**
- **Quicken 4**
- **ToolBook for Windows**
- **Turbo Pascal 5.5**
- **Windows 3.0**
- **Windows 286/386**
- **Word for Windows**
- **WordPerfect 5.1**
- **WordPerfect Library/ Office PC**
- **XTreeGold 2**
- **Your Hard Disk**

Computer users are not all alike. Neither are SYBEX books.

We know our customers have a variety of needs. They've told us so. And because we've listened, we've developed several distinct types of books to meet the needs of each of our customers. What are you looking for in computer help?

If you're looking for the basics, try the **ABC's** series, or for a more visual approach, select **Teach Yourself**.

Mastering and **Understanding** titles offer you a step-by-step introduction, plus an in-depth examination of intermediate-level features, to use as you progress.

Our **Up & Running** series is designed for computer-literate consumers who want a no-nonsense overview of new programs. Just 20 basic lessons, and you're on your way.

SYBEX **Encyclopedias** provide a comprehensive reference and explanation of all of the commands, features and functions of the subject software.

Sometimes a subject requires a special treatment that our standard series doesn't provide. So you'll find we have titles like **Advanced Techniques, Handbooks, Tips & Tricks**, and others that are specifically tailored to satisfy a unique need.

You'll find SYBEX publishes a variety of books on every popular software package. Looking for computer help? Help Yourself to SYBEX.

For a complete catalog of our publications:

SYBEX Inc.
2021 Challenger Drive, Alameda, CA 94501
Tel: (415) 523-8233/(800) 227-2346 Telex: 336311
Fax: (415) 523-2373

Up & Running with Clipper® 5.01

Richard Frankel

SYBEX®

San Francisco ▪ Paris ▪ Düsseldorf ▪ Soest

Acquisitions Editor: David Clark
Series Editor: Joanne Cuthbertson
Editor: Savitha Varadan
Technical Editor: Sheldon Dunn
Word Processors: Ann Dunn, Susan Trybull
Book Designer: Elke Hermanowski
Icon Designer: Helen Bruno
Screen Graphics: Cuong Le
Desktop Production Artist: Helen Bruno
Proofreader: Elizabeth Chuan
Indexer: Ted Laux
Cover Designer: Archer Design
Screen reproductions produced by XenoFont.

Library of Congress Card Number: 91-65513
ISBN: 0-89588-693-6

Manufactured in the United States of America
10 9 8 7 6 5 4 3 2 1

SYBEX Up & Running Books

Who this book is for

The Up & Running series of books from SYBEX has been developed for committed, eager PC users who would like to become familiar with a wide variety of programs and operations as quickly as possible. We assume that you are comfortable with your PC and that you know the basic functions of word processing, spreadsheets, and database management. With this background, Up & Running books will show you in 20 steps what particular products can do and how to use them.

What this book provides

Up & Running books are designed to save you time and money. First, you can avoid purchase mistakes by previewing products before you buy them—exploring their features, strengths, and limitations. Second, once you decide to purchase a product, you can learn its basics quickly by following the 20 steps—even if you are a beginner.

Contents & structure

The first step usually covers software installation in relation to hardware requirements. You'll learn whether the program can operate with your available hardware as well as various methods for starting the program. The second step often introduces the program's user interface. The remaining 18 steps demonstrate the program's basic functions, using examples and short descriptions.

Special symbols and notes

A clock shows the amount of time you can expect to spend at your computer for each step. Naturally, you'll need much less time if you only read through the step rather than complete it at your computer.

You can also focus on particular points by scanning the short notes in the margins and locating the sections you are most interested in.

In addition, three symbols highlight particular sections of text:

The Action symbol highlights important steps that you will carry out.

The Tip symbol indicates a practical hint or special technique.

The Warning symbol alerts you to a potential problem and suggestions for avoiding it.

We have structured the Up & Running books so that the busy user spends little time studying documentation and is not burdened with unnecessary text. An Up & Running book cannot, of course, replace a lengthier book that contains advanced applications. However, you will get the information you need to put the program to practical use and to learn its basic functions in the shortest possible time.

We welcome your comments

SYBEX is very interested in your reactions to the Up & Running series. Your opinions and suggestions will help all of our readers, including yourself. Please send your comments to: SYBEX Editorial Department, 2021 Challenger Drive, Alameda, CA 94501.

Preface

There are many choices in the highly competitive world of PC database products. With the release of version 5.0, Clipper's first major upgrade in over three years, Nantucket Corporation has dramatically improved its database development package in terms of performance, capability, and ease of use. And with version 5.01, Nantucket has improved both the stability and functionality of Clipper. But the immediate questions one asks are: What's the big deal about Clipper? What does it do? And how can this book help me?

WHAT IS CLIPPER?

Pure and simple, Clipper is a database programming language, complete with all the tools necessary to develop stand-alone database applications. As Clipper was originally based on Ashton-Tate's dBASE series, many dBASE programs will be compatible with Clipper with little modification. You might think of Clipper as a superset of the dBASE "language."

Clipper is easy enough that even a novice programmer can use it to develop fast, powerful applications. Those familiar with dBASE III should be able to start creating Clipper applications within a day. Programmers experienced in other languages will find Clipper surprisingly mature (in many ways it is very similar to modern C implementations), and the ideal environment for the rapid creation of database applications. If you need elegant interfaces, then you will be pleased with Clipper's database creation utility (DBU) and source code debugger (CLD).

WHY IS CLIPPER SO GREAT?

Clipper is an excellent choice for database application development for three main reasons: speed, flexibility, and security.

The Speed of a Compiler

Clipper's original reason for coming into existence was the need for a dBASE-compatible compiler. Ashton-Tate's dBASE series, while very useful programs, tended to run excruciatingly slowly for very large databases. The reason for this is that programs written with these products are *interpreted.* When an interpreted program is run, the computer must convert every line of program code into machine language, one at a time, as it is executed. While this gives you the advantage of immediately being able to see your code execute, it can be very slow.

The solution to this torpor is to *compile* all your program code into machine language before execution. Then, when you run your program, it will seem lightning-quick. Clipper compiles its own dBASE "dialect" code into very fast applications. Typically, one should expect speed improvements in searches, sorts, filters, and so forth of as much as ten to twenty times. That's a big difference—you'd spend only five minutes instead of an hour and a half on some jobs.

The Flexibility of a High-Level Programming Language

Since you are writing *all* the code for an application with Clipper, you are in total control. The interface will work the way you want. The menus will be structured as you see fit. If you want to change, modify, or add a feature to your software, you can do it. Great, you may think, but do I have to write thousands of lines of code? Well, no, not necessarily. This is why Clipper is a *high-level* programming language. It has a large number of functions and commands (over three hundred in version 5.01) that are designed specifically with database application creation in mind. While most of the time you will use only fifteen or twenty of these commands, if you need to do something more complex, most likely you can do it in five to ten lines of code rather than a hundred.

Security

Any application developed with Clipper produces a completely independent, executable (.EXE) program. That means that you can write a program and then install it on a hundred PCs *without* having to install Clipper on each and every work station and without infringing upon any copyrights. You can develop an application with Clipper (just as you would with C, Pascal, or BASIC) and sell it without owing any royalties to Nantucket. And finally, your software is protected. Once it is compiled into machine code, nobody can look at and reuse pieces of your programs.

WHY *UP AND RUNNING WITH CLIPPER 5.01*?

As mentioned above, Clipper is big and potentially complicated. But it does not need to be. Most Clipper programs can be written with a very small subset of the commands and features that are available. Certainly you do not need to understand every option of every obscure function to start creating applications with Clipper. That's where this book comes into play. *Up and Running with Clipper 5.01* covers all the major features of Clipper, without choking you on unnecessary detail. This book can serve as a guide for both versions 5.0 and 5.01; any differences between the versions will be discussed when appropriate. If you are a beginning programmer, pay close attention to the early Steps. If you are more experienced, pick and choose, and learn what you need to create your software.

CLIPPER'S ONLINE HELP

Clipper comes with an online help system that will be installed automatically along with the rest of Clipper in Step 1. Once installed, you can load it into memory by typing NG at your DOS prompt. To activate it, press the Shift-F1 key combination. If you do not like the online help or find that it takes up too much memory, you can always uninstall it.

CONVENTIONS USED IN THIS BOOK

The following symbols and conventions are used for Clipper commands and functions throughout this book:

<>	These symbols indicate an item that the user defines or inputs.
[ ]	Brackets surround optional clauses or commands.
¦	This indicates two or more mutually exclusive options.
READ	All Clipper commands and functions are upper case.
ON ¦ off	When more than one option is allowed, the default is always capitalized.
Tot_Sales	All user-defined variables and function/procedure names are italicized.

Table of Contents

60

Installation and Configuration

As with all software, you begin by installing the Clipper files onto your hard disk. This is accomplished with Nantucket's easy-to-use INSTALL program. Once the software is copied to your hard disk, you must configure your hardware to work most efficiently with Clipper. The performance of these tasks for both versions 5.0 and 5.01 is outlined in this Step.

HARDWARE AND SOFTWARE REQUIREMENTS

Clipper requires an IBM-PC or a 100% compatible clone and the following hardware and software components:

- DOS version 3.1 or later.
- 512K RAM, although applications of any significant size will be much easier to run in 640K RAM.
- At least one 5¼ or 3½ inch floppy disk drive.
- A hard disk with at least 1.5 MB of free space for the bare-bones installation. However, I strongly recommend that you install all of Clipper. Version 5.0 requires 5.1 MB of hard disk space; version 5.01 requires about 6 MB of free space.

Of course, you will need additional space for the applications you develop.

- At least 400K of free RAM.

USING THE VERSION 5.0 INSTALL PROGRAM

Installation, while somewhat slow, is almost entirely automated, except for a few decisions that you must make at the start of the process. INSTALL will create a directory structure for the Clipper files, and then copy them to their appropriate locations. Your most difficult task will be to decide on the base directory for the files; your most tedious one will be to swap the disks as prompted.

Follow these steps to install the Clipper files:

1. Insert Clipper 5.0 Disk 1 in drive A.
2. Type **A:** and press Enter to go to drive A.
3. Type **Install** and press Enter.
4. Read the welcome message and then press any key.

Specifying Clipper files' location

By default, Clipper 5.0's base directory is C:\CLIPPER5. If you prefer a different directory, follow steps five and six:

5. Type **P** and press Enter. Press Enter again to get past the source path, assuming that it is still A:.
6. Now type the new path name (for example, **D:**\) and press Enter.

Since INSTALL always appends *\CLIPPER5* to the end of the target path you specify, do not include it in your path. Now, you are ready to actually perform the installation.

7. Continue the installation by typing **C** and pressing Enter.
8. INSTALL will respond with

   ```
   Proceed with Install?y
   ```

   to which you can respond by again pressing Enter.

9. When prompted, insert the indicated disks, pressing Enter after each disk.

There is a minor omission in the Clipper 5.0 INSTALL program that you need to correct now. After creating the applications mentioned above, INSTALL did not copy them to the \CLIPPER5\BIN directory—the directory in which all of your Clipper tools will reside. You should do that now by typing the following DOS commands. If you have changed the default directory for your Clipper files, you should change these commands accordingly.

```
Copy C:\CLIPPER5\SOURCE\PE\*.EXE
C:\CLIPPER5\BIN
Copy C:\CLIPPER5\SOURCE\DBU\*.EXE
C:\CLIPPER5\BIN
Copy C:\CLIPPER5\SOURCE\RL\*.EXE
C:\CLIPPER5\BIN
```

CONFIG.SYS and AUTOEXEC.BAT in version 5.0

INSTALL's final operation was to analyze your CONFIG.SYS and AUTOEXEC.BAT files. It did not change them; instead, it created two files called CONFIG.CHG and AUTOEXEC.CHG in the root directory of the current hard drive (the drive into which the Clipper files were copied). The installation is now complete, so it is up to you to modify your CONFIG.SYS and AUTOEXEC.BAT according to the contents of the .CHG files; see the discussion below.

USING THE VERSION 5.01 INSTALL PROGRAM

Clipper 5.01's INSTALL program is even more automated and easy to use than version 5.0's. Here is what you have to do:

1. Insert Clipper 5.01 Disk 1 in drive A.
2. Type **A:**, and press Enter; then type **Install** and press Enter at your DOS prompt to start the program.
3. Select the target drive (i.e., C or D).
4. Select the target base directory.
5. Select which files to install; press Enter to install all files.

6. Select which utilities to install; press Enter to install all utilities.
7. Insert the indicated disks as requested.
8. Let the program modify your AUTOEXEC.BAT and CONFIG.SYS (see below).
9. Watch INSTALL create the standard Clipper utilities.

Version 5.01 installation errors

If INSTALL fails to create one or more of the Clipper utilities because of a lack of memory or hard disk space, do not despair; you do not have to repeat the entire installation. Instead, free up some more disk space (or memory), then run the INSTALL program and select for installation only those utilities that failed the first time around.

CONFIG.SYS and AUTO-EXEC.BAT files in version 5.01

Unlike version 5.0, the version 5.01 INSTALL program makes direct changes to your CONFIG.SYS and AUTOEXEC.BAT files. You will still need to check these changes, however. Also, you will probably need to add (or modify) the CONFIG.SYS SHELL command as discussed below.

CONFIGURING YOUR PC RUNTIME ENVIRONMENT

Configuring your workstation runtime environment for Clipper will require modification of your AUTOEXEC.BAT and CONFIG.SYS files. To implement or check INSTALL's changes to these files, you should use a file editor such as Clipper's PE (discussed in the next Step).

Configuring Your CONFIG.SYS File

As I mentioned above, Clipper 5.0 suggests changes to be made to your CONFIG.SYS file; these suggestions are contained in a file that you will find in your root directory called CONFIG.CHG. Clipper 5.01's INSTALL makes these changes directly to your CONFIG.SYS.

FILES and BUFFERS settings

Most likely your computer already has a CONFIG.SYS, with FILES and BUFFERS settings determined by software you have installed previously. That's fine—Clipper's suggested values of FILES=21 and BUFFERS=8 are minimums; if your FILES and BUFFERS are set higher, just leave them alone.

There is one additional change you will probably need to make to your CONFIG.SYS. In your AUTOEXEC.BAT you will have a number of SET commands that load information called *environment variables* (including your machine's path) into the DOS environment space. Clipper requires so many of these environment variables for smooth operation that you will probably exceed DOS's default environment space (a mere 160 *bytes* in version 3.2). You will know that this has happened if, when your computer is initializing, you get the message

```
Out of environment space
```

and if your environment variables are not assigned. You can check which ones have been assigned by typing **Set** at your DOS prompt.

DOS version 3.1

Unfortunately, there is no way to increase your environment space with DOS versions prior to 3.2. If you are using version 3.1 and can upgrade, do so. I recommend version 3.3—it is very stable. If you cannot upgrade, you have no choice but to use a short path name and a limited number of SET commands. The most crucial Clipper environment variables are CLIPPER and LIB; try to get at least those two into your environment space. The only way to test if your SETs worked is by changing AUTOEXEC.BAT, rebooting, and watching for *Out of environment space* messages. You may have to repeat the process a few times. Leaving out a few SET variables will not impair the functioning of Clipper; however, you may have to respond to file location queries during compiles or links.

DOS versions 3.2 and later

With DOS versions 3.2 and later, the default environment space can be changed with the SHELL command. To do this, add the following line to your CONFIG.SYS:

The DOS SHELL command

```
SHELL=COMMAND.COM /P /E:500
```

It is crucial that you type the line exactly as it appears here. This command tells your computer to load COMMAND.COM as the operating system. The /P parameter makes this change permanent. The /E parameter defines the environment space to be 500 bytes (not kilobytes!), which is plenty large for the Clipper environment variables and a long path. The maximum value is 32,768, but remember that this is space that comes out of your base 640K RAM memory, so you will want to keep this value as small as possible.

Configuring AUTOEXEC.BAT in Version 5.0

The AUTOEXEC.CHG generated by INSTALL will look like the following:

```
SET PATH=C:\CLIPPER5\BIN;
SET INCLUDE=C:\CLIPPER5\INCLUDE;
SET LIB=C:\CLIPPER5\LIB;
SET OBJ=C:\CLIPPER5\OBJ;
SET CLIPPER=F21;
```

Updating your path

Since you probably have a path command in your AUTOEXEC.BAT already, just add the Clipper path information to the end of your current path. For example, if the current path is

```
PATH=C:\;C:\DOS;C:\WP51;
```

you can change it to

```
PATH=C:\;C:\DOS;C:\WP51;C:\CLIPPER5\BIN;C:\NG;
```

The *C:\NG;* is the path for Clipper's online help.

SET commands

The other four lines of AUTOEXEC.CHG can just be added to your AUTOEXEC.BAT. If you have a menuing program executing last in your AUTOEXEC.BAT, be sure to put the Clipper SET commands before that line. The SET INCLUDE, LIB, and OBJ commands will tell Clipper's compiler and linker where to look for certain files that are necessary for creating Clipper applications. The SET CLIPPER=F21; command tells Clipper the maximum number of file handles available (one for each allowable open file). Twenty-one is enough for most applications, though you can change the number later if you need to have more open files.

Configuring AUTOEXEC.BAT with Version 5.01

Clipper 5.01's installation utility will correctly update your PATH command (with \CLIPPER5\BIN; and \NG;) and automatically add all but one of the SET commands to your AUTOEXEC.BAT file. You will have to add SET CLIPPER=F21; yourself; to do so, follow the steps in the last section. I only found one glitch in this part of the 5.01 INSTALL program. Instead of adding only the SET commands that were needed, INSTALL added them all to the end of my AUTOEXEC.BAT, thus duplicating the Clipper SET commands my AUTOEXEC.BAT already contained. If this happens to you, delete the duplicate SET commands; they will not hurt anything, but they will make your AUTOEXEC.BAT harder to understand.

Once you have made these changes to your AUTOEXEC.BAT and CONFIG.SYS, you have finished modifying your computer's configuration for Clipper. Go ahead and reboot your computer (by pressing Ctrl-Alt-Del). Watch the messages that are typed on the screen during the execution of your AUTOEXEC.BAT. If you see *Out of environment space,* you need to increase the value for the /E parameter of the SHELL command in your CONFIG.SYS as discussed above.

15

PE: The Program Editor

PE.EXE is a simple source code editor supplied with Clipper. It allows you to create and modify ASCII files such as program source code or your AUTOEXEC.BAT or CONFIG.SYS files. If you already have a favorite text editor, you should use it and skip this Step. If not, you can learn from this Step how to use the Clipper Program Editor.

STARTING THE PROGRAM EDITOR

If you followed the installation directions in Step 1, the Program Editor should be in your CLIPPER5\BIN subdirectory, which is included in your path. Now you can invoke the Program Editor from any subdirectory. For example, type

```
PE AUTOEXEC.BAT
```

and press Enter.

You will now see a window with your AUTOEXEC.BAT ready for editing. Any text-only file can be edited with the Program Editor, and file names can include drive, path, and/or extension. Thus, you could have typed

```
PE C:\AUTOEXEC.BAT
```

to get the same result. If the file name you type after PE does not exist in the current directory, PE will create a new file with that name and show you an empty editing window. If you do not specify an extension, PE will assume .PRG. According to the Clipper documentation, if you hit Enter without following "PE" with a file name at the DOS prompt, the Program Editor will ask you for the name of a file to edit. However, this is incorrect—instead, the program will simply create a file called UNTITLED and then present you with an empty editing window. If this happens, you can quit or you can continue editing anyway and change the file name later. How to do this, as well as how to use the other editing capabilities of the Program Editor, will be discussed next.

EDITING

Upon starting the Program Editor, you are shown an editing window that contains one screenful of your selected file. At the bottom of the window is some information beneath a straight line. PE is a tight-lipped program, but will usually tell you the current row and line number (lower right) and the current file name (lower left). Any editing commands that require input will query you in the lower-left corner of the screen.

Basic editing keys

You can add or modify text by moving the cursor and typing, just as you would with any word processor. You can use the four cursor movement arrows as well as PgUp, PgDn, Home (moves to the beginning of the current line), and End (moves to the end of the current line). In addition, there are special key combinations you can use with the Program Editor, as detailed in Table 2.1.

Key	Action
Alt-W	Save this file and continue.
Alt-S	Search for a text string.
Alt-A	Search again (repeat the last search).
Alt-F	Display the file name.

Table 2.1: Program Editor Editing Keys

Key	Action
Alt-O	Change the name of the file.
Esc	Exit Program Editor.
Ctrl-V, Ins	Toggle insert mode.
Ctrl-PgUp	Move to the beginning of the document.
Ctrl-PgDn	Move to the end of the document.
Ctrl-Y	Remove the current line.
Ctrl-T	Delete the word to the right.
Ctrl-←	Move the cursor one word to the left.
Ctrl-→	Move the cursor one word to the right.
Alt-X	Same as Esc. (Version 5.01 only.)
Ctrl-W	Save file and exit. (Version 5.01 only.)
Alt-H, F1	Display Help. (Version 5.01 only.)

Table 2.1: Program Editor Editing Keys (continued)

The Clipper documentation is not entirely correct about editing keys. The following commands listed in Table 6-1 of the Clipper *Programming and Utilities Guide* do not work in version 5.0: Ctrl-W, Alt-X, F3, F4, F5, and F6. Note also that a few useful commands are not listed in the documentation. These are Alt-S (Search), Alt-A (Search again), and Alt-O (Rename file). In Clipper version 5.01, some of these problems have been corrected. The Ctrl-W and Alt-X commands have been returned to the program. Additionally, two new keys, Alt-H and F1, have been added. These perform the same function: they display on screen all keyboard commands allowed in the Program Editor.

Changing the file name

The Program Editor is very simple and straightforward. You can figure out the use of most of the commands listed on Table 2.1 on your own; however, a few, particularly the undocumented ones, are worth discussing. The Alt-O command is handy if you want to make some changes without altering your original. Whenever you press Alt-O, at the bottom of the screen you will see the prompt:

```
Enter new output file name: Current_file
```

(Current_file is the name of the file you have already loaded into the Program Editor.) Now, if you type in the new file name, and hit Enter, you will see:

```
File: New_file
```

Now you are working on a new file with whatever name you typed at the prompt. Note that the Alt-O key *will not* add a file extension onto your file name and that the act of renaming does not save the new file—you have do that later. But you do have a fresh copy to work with, and you can rest assured that you will not harm or alter your old file.

Search commands

Another useful set of editing keys are Alt-S (*Search*) and Alt-A (*Search again*). They can save a lot of tedious screen scrolling by jumping to the desired place in a file. To execute the Program Editor Search key, press Alt-S. In the bottom-left corner of the screen, you will see

```
Search for:
```

Now type in the text you want to search for and press Enter. Be careful—Search is case-sensitive. For example, if you type "Set Path," the search will not find "SET PATH" or "set path." If the search text is found, the cursor will move to the selected text, and the following message will appear in the lower-left corner of the screen:

```
Search completed.
```

If the search is not successful, you will instead see

```
Pattern not found.
```

Now the slick part: If the search was successful, you can press Alt-A, and the program will search again for the same text. You can repeat the Alt-A command until the bottom of the file is reached.

Insert mode

The Program Editor's *insert mode* is similar to that of most word processors, with a few exceptions. You toggle insert mode by pressing the Ins key, or by pressing the Ctrl-V key combination. With insert mode off (the default), text is overwritten as you type. With insert mode on, text (beginning with the character above the cursor) is pushed to the right as you type, making room for the newly typed text. The only way to tell if you are in insert mode is by looking carefully at your cursor. With insert mode *off,* the cursor is only one line thick. When you press the Ins key to enter insert mode, the cursor changes to about the size of a lower case "e." Try pressing the Ins key a few times, and you will see the cursor shrink and grow.

The trickiest thing about insert mode is the Enter key. In insert mode, the Enter key acts as it would in a word processor: Pressed at the end of a line it will give you a new blank line; in the middle of a line it will break the line at the cursor, bring the text to the right of the cursor to the beginning of the next line, and push everything below it down a line. With insert mode off, however, the Enter key will not break the line and will not add a new line—it will merely move the cursor to the beginning of the next line, without affecting the text. This is weird, but you will get used to it quickly. Actually, this function is quite useful, as it is the only way to get quickly to the beginning of the next line of a file.

EXITING THE PROGRAM EDITOR

Saving edited files

Saving your work is very easy. The Alt-W key combination quickly writes your changes to your file. When you are ready to leave the program, press Esc in version 5.0 or Alt-X in version 5.01. The Program Editor is smart enough to check for modifications, and will prompt you if any changes have been made, then try to exit by asking

```
Abandon Current_file [ynw]?
```

Current_file is the file you are working on. The cryptic *[ynw]* is the set of choices you are allowed. These are your options:

- Pressing Y will quit the program and *not* write your modifications to the file. This is the way to lose your work, so be careful!

- Pressing N will return you to the Program Editor. Choose N if you are not finished editing.
- Pressing W will save changes to your file, then quit the Program Editor.

If you have not made any changes to the file, pressing Esc will immediately quit the Program Editor and return you to DOS.

In version 5.01, you are given another way to save your file and exit. The command Ctrl-W performs both these operations: It automatically saves your current file and then exits the Program Editor. This is handy if you want to save and exit quickly. However, you must be careful! This command does not give you the opportunity to change your mind, as Esc and Alt-X do. Once you press Ctrl-W, your file is saved and the old version is overwritten.

THE PROGRAM BEHIND THE PROGRAM EDITOR

If you are interested in the details of how the Program Editor works, you are in luck. Like many of the Clipper 5.0 utilities, PE was written in Clipper, and the source code is sitting on your hard disk. If you installed the default Clipper configuration, the source code for the Program Editor, PE.PEG, is located in the \CLIPPER5\SOURCE\PE directory. You can examine the source code and use it as a model for your own applications, and you can even modify the code to expand the capabilities of the Program Editor to suit your needs.

30

Compiling Clipper Programs

One of the crucial components of the Clipper development environment is its compiler, which is called, not surprisingly, CLIPPER.EXE. Every program you create will have to be compiled, probably many times, until you get it perfect. This Step will discuss what the compiler does, how it does it, and how best to use it.

COMPILER BASICS

The Clipper compiler converts source (.PRG) files containing any number of user-written procedures and functions into object (.OBJ) files. These object files can then be linked with other Clipper object files to form an executable (.EXE) file. Source files containing code to be compiled by Clipper do not have to have .PRG extensions, but as conventions go, this is a useful one. Some examples of file names are MENU.PRG or REPORT.PRG. Naming your source files with consistent extensions will make them easier to find on your hard disk, and Clipper tools such as PE and the compiler will automatically supply the .PRG extension for input files, thus saving you the trouble of typing source extensions every time you use one of those programs.

Compiler error checking

If the compiler just converted source code into machine code, it would not be very useful. What would happen if the program contained an error? Fortunately, one of the major jobs of the Clipper compiler is error checking. The compiler checks to make sure that you use your variables the way you declare them, that you get Clipper's syntax correct, and that you do not abuse a vast host of details. A single misplaced comma or parenthesis could cause your program not to compile. If you are very clever, you can get errors past the compiler, but there are additional stages of application development in which they will (hopefully) be caught. And, of course, just because your program compiles without defect does not mean that it will do what you want it to do. So write your code carefully!

INVOKING THE CLIPPER COMPILER

If you followed the installation procedures in Step 1, you should be ready to compile. If you are not sure about your installation, the compiler-critical steps, other than actually loading the Clipper files onto your hard disk, are the following:

- Adding the \CLIPPER5\BIN directory to your DOS Path.
- Executing SET INCLUDE = C:\CLIPPER5\INCLUDE, hopefully from your AUTOEXEC.BAT file.

There is no need to worry about this if you are using Clipper 5.01. Its installation program will have performed these two steps automatically. Okay—to compile a Clipper .PRG source file, simply enter at the DOS prompt

```
CLIPPER <fn>
```

where *<fn>* is the name of your source file. As mentioned above, if no extension is given, CLIPPER.EXE will assume .PRG. So, to compile the file SAMPLE.PRG, you would type

```
CLIPPER SAMPLE
```

Let's try a very simple bit of code to see how the compiler responds. If you are using Clipper's Program Editor, enter at the DOS prompt

```
PE SAMPLE
```

to enter the editing program. You should see a blank editing window. Note that I did not instruct you to type any extension for the file SAMPLE; this is because PE will automatically add the .PRG extension to the file as it is created. Next, type in these lines, exactly as they appear below:

```
/*  Sample Program  */
??'I wish we would get to real programming.'
```

Although this is not a terribly interesting program, it does teach two simple Clipper commands. The first is the *comment*. The characters /* and */ bracket comments in Clipper, a convention that should look familiar to C programmers. The double question mark displays values to your computer console. The character values after the ?? must be contained in single quotes—that is how Clipper knows they are character values and not Clipper commands. There will be much more on Clipper commands in later Steps. After you have typed in this code, if you are using the Program Editor, press Esc to quit the program. Now respond to

```
Abandon sample.prg [ynw]?
```

by pressing **W** to save your file and quit the program. If you are using a different text editor, enter the lines above and save your file.

To compile, enter the following command at the DOS prompt:

```
CLIPPER SAMPLE
```

The Clipper 5.01 compiler will respond with:

```
Clipper (R)  Version 5.01
Copyright (c) Nantucket Corp 1985 - 1991. All
Rights Reserved.
Microsoft C Floating Point Support Routines
Copyright (c) Microsoft Corp 1984 - 1987. All
Rights Reserved.
302K available
Compiling SAMPLE.PRG
Code size 39, Symbols 48, Constants 41
```

The legal notices are longer than the program! Did you notice something flash by on the line beneath *Compiling SAMPLE.PRG*? That was the compiler counting lines. In a longer program, you would see the compiler at work as it counted the lines, one hundred at a time.

COMPILER OPTIONS

Flexibility is built into the Clipper compiler in the form of a number of options. These options control the behavior of the compiler in a variety of ways, some of which are very useful, some of which border on the arcane. I will discuss only the most valuable of these options, as well as the two methods of specifying them.

Rich Frankel's Favorite Clipper Compiler Options

Unless you are doing some very strange things with your variables, or you are using pre-processor directives (if you have no idea what those are, don't worry about it!), you can probably get by with a small handful of the Clipper compiler options. I will discuss five of them here; for the brave, there are eleven more for version 5.0 and twelve more for version 5.01 described in your Clipper *Programming and Utilities Guide*. For now, trust me, these five will be sufficient for a long time.

/B   Include debugging information

This option tells the compiler to include lots of debugging information about your file, including variable and source file names. When you are ready to start debugging, you must compile your files with this option for the debugger to be at all useful. When your program works perfectly, however, remember to recompile without this option—this will reduce your final executable file size dramatically.

/L   Suppress line numbers

This is an option you will want to use when you are ready for your final compile. It tells the compiler to do its job without including source code line numbers in the object file, thus reducing the object file by three bytes per line of code. Do not compile uncompleted code with this option! If you do, CLIPPER.EXE will not report the line number of errors it encounters, and the debugger will be just about worthless.

/M   Ignore unresolved external references

Now here's an option I use every single time I compile a file. The component procedures of any large program are going to be broken down into small files, for a number of reasons that I will discuss in another Step. These procedures then call upon each other to perform their own specific tasks. Whenever you compile a file that contains calls to procedures outside of that file, the compiler dutifully goes out looking for it, most likely resulting in confusion and ugly errors. The way around this is simply to tell the compiler not to worry about references to external procedures. That is what this compiler option does. Have no fear—all external references will be resolved when you link your object files together.

/O   Compile to an object file or directory

Normally CLIPPER.EXE compiles your .PRG to a file in the current directory with the same name, plus a .OBJ extension. This option allows you to compile to a file with a different name, or if you specify a path ending with a backslash (\), the .OBJ will be written to your selected directory. This option is useful if you need to keep a tight rein over where your object files are stored. See the example in the next section.

/S   Check source code syntax

This command is useful in the beginning stages of program development. It will check the syntax of your .PRG file without taking the time to generate an object file.

Now that you have seen my five favorite options (they are literally the only ones I use 99 percent of the time), it is time to learn how to employ them.

Specifying Options on the CLIPPER.EXE Command Line

By far the most common way in which compiler options are activated is by listing them on the CLIPPER.EXE command line. For example, if you wanted to compile SAMPLE.PRG with the /B option, when compiling the program, you would type

```
CLIPPER SAMPLE /B
```

at the DOS prompt. The syntax rules for compiler options are as follows:

- Options can be in either upper- or lowercase.
- Options must be prefaced by either a slash (/) or a hyphen (-).
- Options may be listed in any order.
- Options must be separated by at least one space.
- Options with arguments must have no spaces between the option character and its arguments.

These may seem like a lot of rules, but by the end of the next Step you will know how to avoid much tedious retyping of the same compile commands. Here is an example of a compile command that combines many of the compiler options. Go ahead and try it on your computer. If you selected a different default location for the \CLIPPER5\ directory, modify the command appropriately.

```
CLIPPER SAMPLE /B /M /OC:\CLIPPER5\OBJ\
```

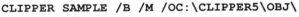

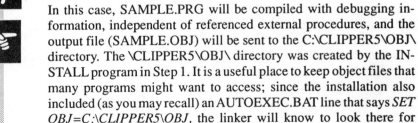

In this case, SAMPLE.PRG will be compiled with debugging information, independent of referenced external procedures, and the output file (SAMPLE.OBJ) will be sent to the C:\CLIPPER5\OBJ\ directory. The \CLIPPER5\OBJ\ directory was created by the INSTALL program in Step 1. It is a useful place to keep object files that many programs might want to access; since the installation also included (as you may recall) an AUTOEXEC.BAT line that says *SET OBJ=C:\CLIPPER5\OBJ*, the linker will know to look there for object files that are not found in the current directory.

In this Step, you have learned how to compile Clipper source files, what the basic options are, and how to specify them. But how do you keep track of your compiles when you are developing a complex application involving many source files? Happily, Clipper provides a utility, RMAKE.EXE, that will make multiple compiles a breeze. And guess what? RMAKE.EXE is the topic of the next Step.

15

Using Clipper's Make Utility

RMAKE.EXE is Clipper's *make facility,* a tool that simplifies the management of applications that are comprised of many files. Generally, a make facility compares the time and date stamps of related files, then performs a series of user-specified actions if those stamps do not match. Specifically, RMAKE will check if your source files are more recent than their compiled (object file) cousins, and compile them if they are. What makes this so useful is that, with one command, you can instruct the computer to compile only those files that have changed since the last make command was issued.

As with most Clipper utilities, RMAKE is delightfully overpowered. To use RMAKE effectively, however, you need only to understand its essential elements: the make file, comments, dependency rules, inference rules, and macros. A discussion of these topics, with examples, will close the subject of compiling.

THE MAKE FILE

The central element of Clipper's make system is the make file. Like source files, make files must be ASCII files, which you can create with any text editor, including Clipper's Program Editor. All make files should have the extension .RMK. The make file defines which files could require updating, the conditions for updating, and what to do when updating is required. Make files are comprised of comments, dependency rules, and inference rules.

Comments in the Make File

The more comments you put in your make file now, the happier you will be when you need to modify it later. There are two kinds of comments allowed for make files:

The two kinds of make commands

- For C aficionados, you can use the form /*...*/, in which your comments take the place of the three dots.
- The characters // can be used for single line comments. No comment-end designator is required.

For example, you might write the following comments:

```
/*  This comment line is legal. */
SAMPLE.OBJ: SAMPLE.PRG  /*  Another legal
comment. */
  Clipper SAMPLE.PRG
// Still another acceptable comment.
```

Dependency Rules

The bulk of your make files will be made up of *dependency rules,* essentially conditions (called *dependency statements*) followed by one or more DOS commands (called *actions*). The syntax of dependency rules is simple, but inflexible. The syntax of the dependency statement is as follows:

Dependency statement syntax

```
<target file>: <dependent file>
```

The dependency statement will be evaluated as a conditional that tells the computer specifically, "If the time/date of the target file is before that of the dependent file, then do the following action(s)." Typically, the *<dependent file>* is used to create the *<target file>*. The classic dependent-statement pair is a source (.PRG) and its object (.OBJ) file. Note that file extensions are *not* omitted! Finally, if more than one dependent is listed, each must be separated by a space. Let's see an

STEP 4

example:

```
SAMPLE.OBJ: SAMPLE.PRG
```

Yes, that is an entire dependency statement. It says, if SAMPLE.PRG is more recent than SAMPLE.OBJ, then do something. That something is defined in the action immediately following the dependency statement.

Dependency action syntax

The syntax for dependency rule actions is as follows:

- Each action must be on a line by itself and must be indented using spaces or tabs. A blank or non-indented line signals that the actions (and dependency rule) have come to an end.

Complete dependency rule example

Here's an example of a *dependency rule*:

```
SAMPLE.OBJ: SAMPLE.PRG
  CLIPPER SAMPLE
```

Remember, both lines comprise the dependency rule. In this case, the target file is SAMPLE.OBJ; it is dependent upon SAMPLE.PRG. In plain English, this dependency rule says, "If the most recent SAMPLE.PRG is dated after SAMPLE.OBJ, then compile SAMPLE.PRG."

Inference Rules

Dependency rules by themselves are not that valuable. What if you want the same action to be performed on many dependency rules? Well, you use an *inference rule*. Inference rules specify an action (or series of actions) to be performed in conjunction with any number of dependency rules. Here is how the system works: If a dependency statement that requires an action is not immediately followed by an action list, RMAKE will search the make file for an inference rule that matches its target and dependent file extensions, then perform its (the inference rule's) action list on that dependency.

Inference rule syntax

The syntax for an inference statement is as follows:

```
.(dependent extension).(target extension):
```

Note that only file extensions are listed, and that the dependent extension is *before* the target extension (the reverse of dependency statements). Only extensions are used because an inference statement establishes a rule for a general set of dependency statements, not for a specific pair of files. There are no spaces in inference statements. The actions that come after the inference statement are any allowable DOS commands; inference rule action syntax is identical to that of dependency rule actions.

Inference rule example

Here is an example of an inference rule:

```
.prg.obj:
  CLIPPER $* /B
```

If one were to translate this inference rule into English, it would read something like, "Go and look for any .OBJ dependent on a .PRG without an action list. If that .PRG is more recent than the .OBJ, compile the .PRG. Repeat these two steps until the end of the file is reached." The $* is a macro, the topic of our next section.

Using Predefined Macros

RMAKE's macro facility allows you to design dependency and inference rules that use variable information. In other words, you can create a rule that can process a general set of files, rather than one specific file. RMAKE has a number of predefined macros, but I am only going to discuss the most useful one, the **$*** macro. Actually, **$** is the macro expansion command, that is, the command that tells RMAKE that the following characters (until the first space) are a macro. The * is the actual predefined macro. When RMAKE encounters $*, it replaces those symbols with the file name of the current dependency statement target file, without path or extension information.

You now can see how the example from the previous page works. The inference rule *CLIPPER $** is a general action that will be executed for any dependency statement lacking an action, whose target and dependent extensions match those of the inference rule, and whose dependent is more recent than its target. In the next section, you will find a number of examples that demonstrate the abilities of RMAKE.

MAKE FILE EXAMPLES

In this first example, RMAKE would determine if three files had been updated since their last compiles, and if not, would compile them with different options:

```
//  Make file for three Sample files
//Dependency rule for SAMPLE1
SAMPLE1.OBJ: SAMPLE1.PRG
  Clipper SAMPLE1 /M  /*  Compile with the 'M'
option  */
//Dependency rule for SAMPLE2
SAMPLE2.OBJ: SAMPLE2.PRG
/*  Compile with the 'M' option and debugging
information  */
  CLIPPER SAMPLE2 /M /B
//Dependency rule for SAMPLE3
SAMPLE3.OBJ: SAMPLE3.PRG
/*  Compile without external references or
line numbers  */
  CLIPPER SAMPLE3 /M /L
```

You can see from the (admittedly excessive) comments what this make file is doing. Although it is unlikely that you would want to perform this wide a variety of operations in one make file, this example does demonstrate the different ways you could combine dependency statements and actions. Here is a more realistic example:

```
/* File MAK_MAIL.RMK:  Make file for
MAILING.EXE */
// Define the inference rule./
.prg.obj:
  CLIPPER $* /M /B
// List of dependency statements.
```

```
MAILING.OBJ: MAILING.PRG
MENU.OBJ: MENU.PRG
SCREEN.OBJ: SCREEN.PRG
REPORT.OBJ: REPORT.PRG
/*  Dependency statement and action for
creating the .EXE from the object files.  */
MAILING.EXE: MAILING.OBJ MENU.OBJ SCREEN.OBJ
REPORT.OBJ
  RTLINK FILE MAILING,MENU,SCREEN,REPORT
```

The inference rule

In this example, the application MAILING.EXE is composed from four source files. The inference rule at the top will be used for any dependency statements without action lists whose extensions match those of the inference rule. The action of the inference rule is to compile those files with the /M and /B options. Each of the next four dependency statements do not have action lists and their extensions match those of the inference rule, so they will use its action rule.

The dependency rule

The dependency statement that begins with MAILING.EXE is a new dependency rule. It will not use the inference rule because it has its own action. The dependency rule says, "If any of these object files is newer than this executable file, then relink these object files." Thus, if any of the source files for this application were modified, merely by typing **RMAKE MAK_MAIL** at the DOS prompt, you could compile those revised files with the appropriate options, and the application would be linked.

You can see how incredibly useful Clipper's make facility is, especially with an application made up of ten or fifteen source files—you can rebuild your entire load (application) by typing one command! Do not worry about the final step of application construction—linking—as that is the topic of the next Step.

30

Creating Executable Files with RTLINK

Now that we have discussed how to edit and compile files, only one more Clipper tool is needed to create independently executable applications. That tool is Clipper's linker, RTLINK. RTLINK is a complex program, both in terms of what it does and how you can use it. This Step will introduce just the material necessary to understand and use RTLINK competently, but you had better be prepared for some jargon anyway.

LINKER BASICS

What RTLINK does

RTLINK combines object (.OBJ) files together with standard libraries to create a stand-alone executable (.EXE) file. You can then run this .EXE file from DOS just as you would any other application by typing its name, followed by a return, at the DOS prompt. Just as CLIPPER.EXE will assume the extension .PRG for its input files, so RTLINK will assume .OBJ.

Dynamic overlays

The key element of RTLINK is its ability to automatically create *dynamic overlays* of Clipper-compiled code, thus allowing programs that are larger than available memory to run. An *overlay* is a small chunk of your program that can be swapped from the hard disk to memory when needed, then back to disk when that section of memory is required for a new chunk. Clipper's overlay manager is called *dynamic* because it determines which chunks are needed as your program is running, as well as where to load them into memory. By default, RTLINK places all the modules in your application into dynamic overlays. For very large or complex applications, other kinds of overlay structures are available, but they are beyond the scope of this book.

INVOKING RTLINK

Although RTLINK allows you the choice of six different styles of input, two will provide all the variety you will *ever* require. This Step will consider the use of RTLINK with two modes of its default FREEFORMAT interface: *Command Line* mode and *Script File* mode. Although some of you may be familiar with the POSITIONAL interface from experience with Microsoft LINK, you should learn FREEFORMAT anyway—it is more flexible *and* more readable.

Invoking RTLINK at the Command Line

RTLINK is started by typing its name at the DOS prompt. In Command Line mode, all the information that RTLINK needs to create an executable file is typed at the DOS prompt as well. The only *required* parameters on the command line are, sensibly enough, the list of object files to be linked. Thus, the format for this command is

```
RTLINK FILE <object file list>
  (OUTPUT <output file name>) (options)
```

where *<objectfile list>* is the list of object files to be linked, separated by commas. For files listed without extensions, .OBJ is assumed. Unless an output file name is specified with the OUTPUT parameter, the executable (.EXE) file created by RTLINK will take the name of the first file in *<objectfile list>*. In addition to the FILE and OUTPUT parameters, there are quite a few link options, two of which will be discussed below. Command line options must be separated by a space and can be placed in any order.

In Step 2, you created and compiled a file called SAMPLE.PRG. Let's try linking that file now. Enter at your DOS prompt:

```
RTLINK FILE Sample
```

You will see a few lines on your screen telling you that the linker is working, and telling you of any errors that RTLINK might find during linking. Assuming that your program linked successfully, only one line of output is interesting. That is the second-to-last line, which should say something like *123K*—the approximate size (123 kilobytes) of your application.

Clipper applications' size

The seemingly excessive size of this application is due to the overhead required for Clipper's dynamic overlays, virtual memory management, and library functions. For large applications, the more memory (including expanded and extended memory) that you have available, the more quickly they will run.

Before we go any further, try running SAMPLE.EXE by typing **Sample** at your DOS prompt and hitting Enter. Congratulations on your first Clipper application!

How RTLINK finds library files

Clipper's standard procedures and functions are contained in a set of libraries that were loaded into the \CLIPPER5\LIB directory of your hard disk during installation. At link time, RTLINK will try to find these libraries so that it can link in the library commands or functions that are needed for your application. It knows where to look for the libraries because of the SET LIB=C:\CLIPPER5\LIB (or the equivalent for your directory structure) that you added to your AUTOEXEC.BAT command back in Step 1. If RTLINK prompted you for the location of the directory containing CLIPPER.LIB, EXTEND.LIB, and TERMINAL.LIB while linking SAMPLE, you must have omitted that step. To avoid a lot of tedium during future links, I strongly suggest that you go back and add your SET commands (see Step 1) to AUTOEXEC.BAT (and reboot your computer) now.

Invoking RTLINK with a Script File

I bet you were wondering what to do if you have a long list of object files to link together, and you want to avoid the annoyance of repeatedly typing lengthy link commands at your DOS prompt. Well, *script files* are the answer. A script file is an ASCII text file that contains a series of link commands. By convention, linker script files have the extension .LNK, which RTLINK will assume if none is specified. You tell RTLINK to use a script file by entering

```
RTLINK @<script file> (options)
```

at the DOS prompt. Do not forget the @! When using script files, RTLINK options can be entered at the command line normally, but command line options will be overridden by contradictory options in your script file.

Script file syntax

The script file itself is just a list of RTLINK arguments and options. The syntax for script files is as follows:

- Valid arguments and options can be placed in any order.
- More than one command can be placed on a line.
- Commands must be separated by at least one space.
- Long commands can be continued on the next line simply by pressing Enter.
- Comments are begun with the # character. The rest of the line after a # is ignored.

Here is an example of a script file for the SAMPLE program; if you want to create it, you can use Clipper's Program Editor by typing

```
PE SAMPLE.LNK
```

at your DOS prompt and then entering the following lines:

```
# Script file for Linking SAMPLE.OBJ
FILE SAMPLE
# Call the output .EXE RUN_SAM.EXE instead of
```

```
#    SAMPLE.EXE
OUTPUT RUN_SAM
```

To save and quit from PE, hit Esc followed by a **w**.

To link with this script file, enter at your DOS prompt:

```
RTLINK @SAMPLE
```

Linking in make files

Notice that the OUTPUT option allowed the executable to be named something other than SAMPLE.EXE. Also note that the line *RTLINK @SAMPLE* could have been placed as the last line of a make file that compiled SAMPLE.OBJ (see Step 4). RMAKE has no trouble executing RTLINK with script files.

RTLINK OPTIONS

As you would expect, RTLINK has many options (over twenty), of which only one is really useful for beginning Clipper programmers.

Using Pre-linked Libraries

After doing a few links, especially on large applications, you will probably begin to notice the length of the process. However, there is a way to speed up linking. Clipper allows you to link commonly used, fixed code into an intermediate file called a *pre-link library,* or .PLL. Then, at link time, RTLINK does not need to link the modules in the .PLL (it's already done), and it does not have to incorporate those pre-linked modules into the final executable file.

Advantages of pre-linking

If SAMPLE.OBJ were linked, with the standard Clipper libraries pre-linked, the resulting executable would have been 4K instead of 130K! Thus, you have two immediate and significant savings: linking is *much* faster, and hard disk space is conserved. The latter is true because any number of executable files can share the same pre-link library, thus making unnecessary the duplication of that library in multiple .EXE's on a single hard disk. Also, you can include pre-link libraries with your distributed .EXE files. Later, if you change the .EXE, you can give your users *just* the updated executable file.

STEP 5

After all that verbiage, you're probably wondering how to use pre-link libraries. All it takes is two steps:

1. Add **Set PLL=C:\CLIPPER5\PLL** to your AUTOEXEC.BAT or enter the Set command at your DOS prompt (in version 5.0 only).
2. Add **/PLL:*<pre-link library name>*** to your script file or RTLINK command line.

The first step tells Clipper where to find your pre-link libraries if they are not in the current directory. The second step specifies which pre-link library to use.

BASE50 and pre-link transfer files

During the Clipper installation, Clipper's standard libraries were pre-linked for you. This pre-linked library is called BASE50.PLL. It is in your /CLIPPER5/PLL directory. Note that BASE50.PLL is accompanied by a file called BASE50.PLT. This is a *pre-link transfer file,* an informational file that is created with every pre-link library. It must be in the same directory as its partner pre-linked library, as it is used by RTLINK whenever that pre-linked library is linked into an executable.

Earlier in this Step, we created an RTLINK script file called SAMPLE.LNK. To modify it to link with BASE50.PLL (the pre-linked standard Clipper libraries), do the following:

1. If you didn't do step 1 above, do so now.
2. Change the fourth line of SAMPLE.LNK from *OUTPUT Run_Sam* to **OUTPUT RUN_SAM /PLL:BASE50.**

After linking (by typing **RTLINK @SAMPLE**), look at the size of your RUN_SAM.EXE file; it should be about 4K. Note that using pre-linked libraries does not affect the performance of Clipper applications; their only purpose is to speed development.

You can also use RTLINK to create pre-linked libraries of your own object files, but that topic is beyond the scope of this book.

Specifying Environmental RTLINK Options

As with the other Clipper tools, you can set RTLINK options in the DOS environment with the RTLINKCMD environment variable. You do this by entering

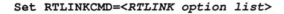

```
Set RTLINKCMD=<RTLINK option list>
```

at your DOS prompt. In my day-to-day Clipper programming, it should come as no surprise that I use

```
Set RTLINKCMD=/PLL:BASE50
```

Of course, this command can be added to your AUTOEXEC.BAT; however, options set in RTLINK command lines or script files will take precedence over those specified with a DOS Set command.

Incremental Linking

I mention incremental linking only to warn you not to bother with it. Supposedly, linking with the /INCREMENTAL option makes RTLINK keep track of which files have been changed since the last link, and only link those that have been modified. The advantage is supposed to be much shorter linking times. Unfortunately, after exhaustive experimentation with this option, I can only conclude that it has no effect on link times. Maybe Nantucket will get it working in a future version of Clipper.

BEYOND THIS STEP

It is possible to link Clipper objects with objects created with other compilers (such as one of the C or ASSEMBLER variants). See *static overlaying* and the EXTEND system in your Clipper documentation for more information.

15

All the Theory You Will Need

Before we can get into the actual details of the Clipper programming language, we must first discuss the essentials of program design. This Step will address such questions as: How should programs be structured and organized? Why is documentation important, and how should it be written? And what are the basic ideas of database programming?

HOW TO BEGIN: AN INTRODUCTION TO PROGRAM DESIGN

A computer program is more than a series of lines of code—it is the detailed expression of the solution to a problem. The problem could be as simple as "How can I create a process to add three numbers together?" or as complex as "How can I automate my company's accounting system?" But knowing you have a problem to solve (or process you want to speed up) is only the beginning. For this discussion, I have reduced the creation of a computer program to four basic phases:

The four phases of programming

- Definition phase
- Design phase

- Programming and documentation phase
- Test phase

Each phase is essential; skipping any would result in wasted time, blown schedules, sleepless nights, and unhappy bosses and customers.

Defining the problem

The better you define your problem at the outset, the fewer hassles you will have later. Carefully *write down,* in as much detail as possible, exactly what you want your program to do. Talk to as many different people about the project as possible, including both managers and end-users. Your client must see *and* approve your clearly detailed proposal before you write a single line of code.

Designing the program

This stage may seem simple, but it is crucial. The program design is essentially an outline: a written listing of all the major sections of the software, grouped under headings. Here is an example of a simple program design for a database used to generate mailing labels for a company's customers.

A. Add customers to the database.

B. Examine and modify the customer data.

C. Delete customer data.

D. Generate mailing labels.

Then, each heading would be fleshed out with additional details. For example, section D might be expanded to:

D. Generate mailing labels.

1. Allow the user to specify zip code ranges for printing.
2. Allow the user to sort the labels by last name.
3. Allow the user to sort the labels by zip code.

Generally, you will know your design is complete when you have no more answers to the question "What else does the user want this program to do?"

Programming and documenting

Once your design is complete, you are ready to begin programming. The two hallmarks of good programming, organization and documentation, will be discussed below.

The test phase

There is no such thing as a perfect program, especially after the first draft. It is crucial that you thoroughly test every detail of your program, in as many combinations as possible. You will be amazed how many typographical errors, lost commas, and incorrectly defined variables will spill from your fingers. And don't forget the screens, menus, and reports that must be fine-tuned until they are just right.

When to test your application

Also, do not wait until you have written every single line of code before you begin testing—correcting an error in ten lines of code will be much, much easier than correcting one in five hundred lines. You will know you are testing too large sections of code at a time if you have to spend hours just *finding* which line contains the error. Typically, the programming and testing phases will go hand in hand.

MODULAR PROGRAMMING

In the last section, I wrote that one of the hallmarks of programming is organization. Back when you designed your program, you grouped the abilities of the application into sections. In programming, code that is broken down into sections is said to be *modular.* Each section, or *module,* does a specific action and is more or less independent. So when you write an application, you are really writing a collection of short programs that can activate each other, pass information back and forth, and share a collective pool of data (the database).

The value of modules

So why use modules? There are two primary reasons. As I discussed before, finding errors in your software will be much easier if you test small sections at a time. At the end of each module, you will reach a natural point at which you can pause and perform tests. By testing each module as it is written, you can build up a base of code that you know works. The second reason to write modular programs is understandability. When you want to modify your software a year after you have finished the application, understanding very long pieces of code could be quite difficult. If your code is broken up into small, well defined sections, it will be easy to find the piece you want to modify and alter it appropriately.

STEP 6

MENU-DRIVEN APPLICATIONS

If you have used computers, you have probably used programs driven by menus. The advantages of menus are obvious: they make it easy for the user to see both what the program can do, and how to make the program perform its functions. For the programmer, menus help with organization: each selection on a menu can be its own module. With Clipper, it is so easy to create fully menu-driven applications that you have no excuse not to incorporate menus in any application. Step 11 will explain how to program with Clipper's menuing commands.

ON DOCUMENTATION

You might remember that the second hallmark of good programming is documentation. Documenting your code may be dull, but it will help you avoid hours of confusion in the future; if you cannot read your code now, you will certainly not be able to understand it in a year.

Self-Commenting Variables

The simplest way to document your code is by using self-commenting variables. Don't worry, this is just a fancy name for a simple idea: instead of giving your variables names like *x, x1,* and *t,* let your variables describe their purpose. If you have a variable that keeps track of the current line number on a report, call it *line_number.* Call the input from the main menu *main_menu_choice.* You can also create your own conventions for naming variables; for example, all input from a certain data screen could begin with the letter "s": *s_firstname, s_lastname, s_city,* etc.

Comments

The next simple way to document your code is to add *comments.* Comments are nonexecuting lines of code that describe the software around them. Lots of brief comments will dramatically improve your ability to understand your code. Clipper accepts three types of comments:

Types of comments

/* ... */	All code following a /* is ignored by the compiler, including returns, until the corresponding */ is reached. (This is also standard in C programming.) This is useful for multiline comments.
*	Lines with an asterisk in the *first column* will be ignored, as in dBASE programs.
//	The // or && comment can appear anywhere in a line. The compiler will ignore any text after them until the next hard return, just as in make files.

Use of White Space

The final way to make your programs more readable is with judicious use of white space. First, space your code out. There is no reason to cram as many lines of code on the screen as possible. Second, indent liberally, especially to reflect program structure. This idea will become more meaningful in Step 9, where control structures are discussed.

PROGRAMMING WITH DATABASES

Since the heart of Clipper is a programming language specifically designed for manipulating databases, no discussion of programming ideas can be complete without a description of database structures.

Database Files and Structures

Consistent with the dBASE standard, all Clipper databases are given the .DBF extension. The set of field definitions is called the *database structure,* and is stored in the same .DBF file that contains the actual data. It is possible to modify a structure—that is, add, delete, or modify the structure of fields from a database—once it is initially created; however, you must be cautious. Once a field is deleted from a database, the data for that field in each record will be lost forever. How to design a database will be discussed in Step 12.

STEP 6

Indexes, Filters, and Sorts

After you enter a mass of data into a database, you will probably want to be able to look at the data in a particular order (such as alphabetical by last name) or to act on a particular subset of the data (such as all the records in the state of Arizona). Clipper can do both of these tasks.

Sorting

You can alter the order of the records in two basic ways. The more intuitive (and obsolete) method, *sorting,* literally rearranges the records so that they end up in a desired order. However, with not even very large databases, sorting can be a slow process. A database with thousands of records would sort unbearably slowly. As you might have guessed, there is an alternative: *indexing*.

Indexing

When you index a database, Clipper creates a special (.NTX) file that contains a cross-reference for the records in the order desired. As you add and modify records, Clipper automatically updates the index for you. An index for a database is similar in concept to the index of a book. Which is faster—looking on every page of a book for a specific entry, or looking for the reference in an index and then immediately going to the appropriate page? Since you can have many indexes for the same databases, you can effectively change the order of a database immediately by changing the active index. Also, finding a specific record in an indexed database is almost instantaneous. Unless you design your database very poorly, you will never need to use sorting; indexes will solve all your search and sort needs. The mechanics of indexes will be discussed in Step 13.

Filters

Filtering is another useful way to manipulate a database. When you create a filter for a database, you tell the computer that you only want to see records in which a certain field matches a specific criterion. For example, you might want to see only customers whose last names begin with the letter M. Until you release the filter, the database will appear to contain just those records that match the filter condition. The filter is an extremely valuable tool in the arsenal of the database programmer and will be discussed in Step 14.

30

Using Variables in Clipper

As in any programming language, the basic building blocks of Clipper programs are *variables*. This step will discuss the kinds of variables allowed in Clipper, their properties, and the types of data that can be stored in variables.

VARIABLES

The are four basic kinds or *classes* of variables in Clipper 5.01. Two of these, PUBLIC and PRIVATE, date from Clipper Summer '87, and are referred to (for you lovers of jargon) as *dynamically scoped.* This is a fancy term for variables that are created and maintained completely at runtime. Consistent with Nantucket's attempt to make Clipper a more complete, robust, and structured language, this release includes two new classes, STATIC and LOCAL, that are *lexically scoped.* These variables are completely determined at *compile-time*. This means that STATIC and LOCAL variables are much faster than their older dynamically scoped counterparts, and will never cause variable referencing errors at runtime. You should always try to use lexically scoped variables. However, all four kinds of variables will be discussed in this Step.

Variable Basics

There are some basic rules that apply to all variables. Each exists for a different period, depending upon the variable type. All variable declarations must come at the beginning of a procedure or function, that is, before any executable statements. Note that undeclared variables in procedures and functions will default to the PRIVATE class. Every variable is referred to by name, which is established in a variable declaration statement. (Conventions for naming variables were given in Step 6.) You should name your variables carefully: you (and your program) could get confused if the same name is used more than once. Some variable types can be initialized, or given a value, immediately upon declaration. Examples of variable declaration and initialization will follow.

Local Variables

Local variables *must* be declared explicitly in your programs with the LOCAL statement. They are created anew every time their procedure is called, and continue to exist and to be accessible until that procedure is completed, at which time its local variables are destroyed. *Only* the procedure in which the local variables are created can access those variables; procedures or functions that are called by it *do not* have access to its local variables. Here is an example:

```
PROCEDURE My_Proc
  LOCAL Sum, Total := 5
  /*  Executable statements go here  */
RETURN
```

In this procedure, the variables Sum and Total are defined to be local, and Total is initialized with a value of 5. Since Sum was not initialized, it is given a value of NIL (the standard for noninitialized local variables). Remember, since Sum and Total are local variables, any procedures or functions called in My_Proc would not have access to them!

Static Variables

Static variables make up the second class of lexically scoped variables. They are similar to local variables, except that static variables *are not* destroyed when the procedure in which they are declared comes to an end. In fact, static variables are not created the first time their procedure is called; they are created (and initialized) when your application is first executed. They are then available to the procedure that contains the STATIC statement every time it is called.

Static variables must be declared explicitly with the STATIC statement. Static variables declared in the body of a procedure or a function can only be accessed within that function. Like local variables, static variables *are not* accessible to procedures and functions called by the procedure in which the static variables were declared. Noninitialized static variables are given the value NIL. Here is an example:

```
PROCEDURE My_Proc
  STATIC Counter := 0, Print_Status := "ON"
  /*  Executable statements go here  */
RETURN
```

In this example, the variables Counter and Print_Status are declared static. Counter is initialized to 0, Print_Status to ON. Since Counter is a static variable, if it is set to 1 the first time My_Proc is called, the next time My_Proc is activated, Counter will still have 1 as its value. Static variables can be very useful for complex processing tasks.

Private Variables

While variables can be declared as private with the PRIVATE statement, any previously undeclared variable that is assigned a value is automatically created as a private variable. Like local variables, private variables will continue to exist until the procedure in which they are declared (or created) is completed, at which time its private variables will be released from memory. However, unlike local variables, private variables *are accessible* by any and all functions and procedures that are called by the creating procedure. Look at the following example:

```
PROCEDURE My_Proc
  PRIVATE Menu := "FIRST"
  iLoop := 1
  /*  Executable statements go here  */
RETURN
```

In this case, the private variable Menu is declared and given the value FIRST. If iLoop has not been defined or declared previously, then it will be created as a private variable, and the value 1 will be assigned to it. Procedures or functions that are called by My_Proc *would* have access to both Menu and iLoop, as well as to any procedures or functions that they might, in turn, call. Private variables that are declared and not initialized are given the default value NIL.

Public Variables

Public variables are, like private variables, dynamically scoped, andPublic variables are declared using the PUBLIC statement. Any variable assigned as public is initialized upon program execution, and is accessible by *every* function and procedure that comprises the application. Additionally, public variables are never automatically destroyed (released from memory). Noninitialized public variables are given a value of .F. upon declaration. Look at the following example:

```
PROCEDURE My_Proc
  PUBLIC Designer := "Frankel"
  /*  Executable statements go here  */
RETURN
```

In this case, the public variable Designer is created and initialized at the beginning of My_Proc. Any other procedure in the program, whether it is called by or calls My_Proc, can employ or modify Designer.

When Should You Use Which Variable Class?

Generally, you should always try to use local variables. Programs written with local variables will run the fastest and be the easiest to understand and debug. Only procedures with just local variables are truly modular: they depend on no outside information. However, you can use static variables if you need to keep track of some data point through multiple calls of the same procedure. Private variables are handy if you have a complicated tree of procedures that all need access to the same data. Public variables should be used sparingly—they are messy, inefficient, and sometimes confusing. In Step 10, you will find out how to pass variable information between procedures without declaring them as private or public.

FIELD VARIABLES

FIELD variables are a special kind of variable that you will use in your software. They are unique because they do not have to be declared and because they are directly connected to information in a database. For example, if you have an active database with a field called STATE , any time Clipper encounters the variable STATE in your software it will use the information stored in that field in the current record of the current active database. For example, the statement

```
CUR_STATE = STATE
```

will assign the value of the STATE field in the current record of the active database to the variable CUR_STATE. Whenever you want to retrieve information from or store information into a database, you will use field variables.

DATA TYPES

The kind of data that is stored in a variable is called its *data type*. For example, a variable stored with the character string *GoodMorning* is said to have the *Character* data type. A variable stored with the number *5* is said to have the *Numeric* data type. Each of the four storage classes discussed above can contain *any* of the data types, but any single variable can only have one data type at a time. Generally, a variable's data type is determined the first time it receives a value; however, the data type of a variable can be changed. The five most important data types will be discussed here.

The character data type

The *character* data type is used to manipulate strings. Character strings are defined by enclosing a series of characters between a pair of *delimiters*. Clipper has defined three sets of delimiters:

- Two single quotes. Example: 'Kennedy'
- Two double quotes. Example: "Kennedy"
- Left and right brackets. Example: [Kennedy]

Null, or empty, strings can be expressed by a pair of delimiters with no characters in between, for example, "".

The numeric data type

The *numeric* data type is used to define data upon which you want to perform mathematical operations. Numeric data can be defined as positive or negative, and with or without a decimal point. Numeric data is not placed between delimiters—numbers placed between delimiters will be treated as character strings. Here are some examples of acceptable numeric data constants:

- 587
- -587
- 5.891
- -.0432
- +587.0

The first and last examples define the same number.

The logical data type

The logical data type is used to identify data that is Boolean, or that can only have one of two possible values, such as true or false, yes or no, etc. The possible values for logical data are y, Y, t, T, n, N, f, and F. For the purposes of logical data, y, Y, t, and T are equivalent; and n, N, f, and F are equivalent. You define variables as logical by giving them one of these values enclosed between two periods—periods are the delimiters for logical variables. Here are some examples of logical variable assignment:

```
Print_On := .F.
Data_Saved := .y.
Data_Saved := .T.
```

Note that the last two assignments are equivalent.

The date data type

The *date* data type is used to represent calendar dates. It is useful because Clipper includes many functions and operators that allow you to manipulate and compare dates. Dates do not have a simple method of representation like characters or logical data; they must be defined using CTOD(), the convert character to date function. To create a date, you convert a character string (of the form mm/dd/yy, or month/day/year) to a date value. Here are some examples:

```
Cust_date := CTOD("01/12/91")
Cur_date := CTOD('11/06/88')
```

Remember, the date input to the CTOD() function must be defined as a character string!

The NIL data type

Variables that are declared but not initialized are given the *NIL* data type. You can also explicitly define a variable to have the NIL data type by assigning NIL directly to that variable, as follows:

```
Test_value := NIL
```

Note that NIL is *not* delimited! The NIL data type was created for Clipper so that operations or comparisons on undefined variables do not result in runtime errors. Instead of your program dying because it does not know the contents of an undefined variable, it is notified by the NIL value that the variable has no value.

BEYOND THIS STEP

One of Clipper's great strengths is its diversity of data types. There are many operators and functions that can perform actions on each data type. Additionally, it is possible to convert variables from one data type to another. See, for example, CTOD(), VAL(), DTOC(), and CHR() in your Clipper documentation. Clipper provides an especially diverse set of functions for manipulating character and numeric data. For more advanced programming tasks, Clipper also supports *arrays* as data types.

15

Operators and Expressions

Variables by themselves are not terribly useful unless your program can act on them. Clipper supplies a vast number of methods for acting on variables: the most basic are the operators. Operators are used in conjunction with variables, constants, and functions to build Clipper expressions. Expressions will be discussed at the end of this Step.

CLIPPER OPERATORS

Operators are symbols that are used with variables to create expressions. Whether you know it or not, you are already familiar with operators. The mathematical expression 5 + 6 includes the numeric constants, 5 and 6, as well as the addition operator, +. When you see this expression, you know that the addition operator instructs you to add together the numbers to its left and right (its *inputs,* or *operands*).

Clipper provides many operators, but you must use them precisely; depending on its context, a symbol can represent many different operators. Mixing data types in expressions can result in runtime errors. Some operators require one operand (*unary operators*) while others require two (*binary operators*). Careful use of operators will save you time and headaches when you later debug your program. This Step discusses several operators specific to each data type, and then examines more general operators.

STEP 8

Character String Operators

Concatenation operators

The two basic string operators are *concatenators*: they add, or concatenate, strings to each other. Both are binary; that is, they require two character-type operands, and both return a character value. They are:

+ Basic concatenate

– Concatenate without intervening spaces

The – operator moves any spaces at the end of the first operand to the end of the resulting string, thus removing all spaces in between the two input strings. The + operator does not move spaces. Here are some examples of concatenations:

```
LOCAL Name1, Name2
Name1 = "Thomas           " + "Smith"
Name2 = "Thomas           " - "Smith"
```

In these examples, both Name1 and Name2 would contain the concatenation of the two strings, but they look slightly different. Name1 contains the spaces after Thomas because the + operator was used. It would look like "Thomas   Smith". Name2 would look like "ThomasSmith." The operator eliminated all the spaces in the variables. Clearly, neither result would be acceptable. However, you could ensure that a single space separated the two names by writing your code like this:

```
LOCAL Name
Name = "Thomas           " - " " + "Smith"
```

The result of this expression is that Name would contain "Thomas Smith."

The subset operator

A handy character operator is $, the subset operator. It tests whether the expression on its left is a subset of (is contained in) the expression on its right. It is also binary, and gives a logical output. For example,

```
"hog" $ "Warthog"
```

would return a value of .T. The subset operator *is* case sensitive, so if the expression had read *"hog" $ "WartHog"*, it would have returned a value of .F. instead.

Mathematical Operators

Clipper permits standard mathematical operators. Generally, the mathematical operators require numerical data types as operands, are binary, and return a numeric value. The + and – operators can also be used to denote positive or negative values. The mathematical operators are:

+	Addition or unary positive
–	Subtraction or unary negative
*	Multiplication
/	Division
%	Modulus (returns the remainder of a division operation)
** or ^	Exponentiation

Date Operators

The date operators provide the only exceptions to the general rule that data types cannot be mixed in Clipper expressions. The two date operators are + and –. These operators allow you to add or subtract days, in the form of numeric data values, to or from date variables. Here are a few examples:

```
LOCAL Entry_date, Due_date, Billing_date
Entry_date = CTOD("11/27/91")
Due_date = Entry_date + 30
Billing_date = Due_date - 21
```

In these examples, all variables are declared local. *Entry_date* is assigned a value, as was discussed in the last Step. *Due_date* will contain a date value thirty days after that of *Entry_date*. *Billing_date* will contain a date value equivalent to three weeks (twenty-one days) before *Due_date*.

Logical Operators

The three basic logical operators are extremely useful for comparing logical type variables as well as for comparing logical expressions. The logical operators are:

.AND.	Logical and
.OR.	Logical or
.NOT. or !	Logical negate

.AND. and .OR. are binary operators. .NOT. and ! are unary, and perform exactly the same function. The result of a logical operation is always a logical value, that is, .T. or .F. The .AND. operator returns true only if *both* of its operands are true. .OR. returns true if *either* of its operands is true. The .NOT. or ! operator returns true if its operand is false. Note the use of the logical operators in the following example:

```
LOCAL First_pass := .T., Printer_on := .F.,
LOCAL Menu_on := .T.
LOCAL Test1, Test2, Test3, Test4
Test1 = First_pass .AND. Printer_on
  //Result: .F.
Test2 = First_pass .AND. .F.
  //Result: .F.
Test3 = !Printer_on
  //Result: .T.
Test4 = Menu_on .OR. Printer_on
  //Result: .T.
```

Relational Operators

The relational operators allow you to compare variables of the *same data type*. They are all binary, and all return logical values. These operators can be used for *any* data type.

<	Less than
>	Greater than

=	Equal
≠	Not equal
<=	Less than or equal
>=	Greater than or equal

Assignment Operators

Assignment operators are used to assign values to variables. All assignment operators are binary. Each requires a single variable on its left side and either an expression or a simple variable or constant on its right. Generally, the two operands must be of the same data type. While there are many specialized assignment operators, I will discuss only two.

The simple assign operator

The *simple assign* operator, or =, is used to assign a value to a single variable. Note that the = sign also serves as the (relational) equality operator and will be interpreted as such if it occurs in an expression. The = sign is used in both ways in the following example:

```
LOCAL Test1, Test2
Test1 = 7           //= used for a simple assign
?(Test1 = Test2)    //= used to test equality
```

The second line will assign the value 7 to the variable *Test1*. In the last line, however, since the = operator is used in an expression, it will serve as the equality operator. It will evaluate whether or not the two variables, *Test1* and *Test2*, are equal, returning .T. if they are and .F. if they are not.

The in-line assign operator

The *in-line assign* operator can always be used in place of the simple assign. However, it has another function. It can be used to assign a value to a variable anywhere in a command line in which a statement is allowed. The in-line assign must be used, for example, when a variable is initialized in a declaration statement. This operator is also useful for assigning a variable in the middle of a complex expression. See the following example:

```
First_date = ( Entry_date := ;
  CTOD("01/01/92") ) + 14
```

This expression does two major operations: First, it assigns the date 01/01/92 to the variable *Entry_date*. Then it adds 14 to that date, and stores the new value in *First_date*. You should, however, use such complex in-line assignments judiciously; they can make your program incomprehensible.

Operator Precedence

In complex statements involving many operators, the operators are resolved in the following order:

- String
- Date
- Mathematical
- Relational
- Logical
- Assignment

Operations in parentheses are evaluated first. Individual string operators have the same level of precedence, and so are evaluated left to right. The same is true for date and relational operators. Logical operators are evaluated in the following order: negate, and, or. Mathematical operators follow the standard order of operations: first positive and negative; then exponentiation, multiplication, and division; and finally, addition and subtraction. Multiplication and division have the same precedence, as do addition and subtraction.

EXPRESSIONS

An expression written in Clipper is any combination of variables, constants, operators, and functions. Expressions are used to write the "phrases" and "sentences" of your programs. In order for your expressions to compile correctly, the syntax of all of the expression components must be correct. Remember to observe data type consistency—mixing data types in expressions will cause errors. You have already seen examples of expressions in this and preceding Steps. Future Steps will include many more for your perusal.

Continuation

If your expressions run long, you can continue them from one line to the next by using a semicolon. This can make long and confusing lines easier to read and understand, as in the following example:

```
Horse_Age := INT( ;
  ( CTOD("01/01/92") - Horse_birth_date ) ;
  / 365 )
```

What does this line do? Assuming that the variable *Horse_birth_date* is of type date, *CTOD("01/01/92") - Horse_birth_date* determines the number of days between January 1, 1992 and the date value in *Horse_birth_date*. This numeric value is then divided by 365 (the number of days in a year) to get the total number of years, i.e., the horse's age, as of 01/01/92. Finally, the number is converted to an integer value with the INT() function, before being assigned to the variable *Horse_age*.

BEYOND THIS STEP

Of course, there are many more operators available with Clipper. These include more complex assignment operators, increment and decrement operators, the macro operator, and some "special" operators. Some of these will be discussed as they are needed in later Steps.

30

Using Control Structures

How do you write code to execute expressions conditionally, or to execute sets of expressions more than once? A program of even minimal complexity will require such programming structures. Clipper provides a standard implementation of programming control structures with *DO WHILE...ENDDO, IF...ENDIF,* and *DO CASE ...ENDCASE.* These control structures must have a beginning and an end statement, and may be nested within each other. These control structures are essential to writing efficient programs.

LOOPING STRUCTURES

Whenever you want to execute a piece of code more than once, you will use looping structures. You might want to perform a series of operations on every record in a database in a particular state. Putting the code in a loop would be the efficient way to solve the problem.

DO WHILE...ENDDO Loops

The most common looping structure is *DO WHILE...ENDDO.* It performs the set of instructions in between the *DO WHILE* and the *ENDDO* until a specified condition is no longer true. For example,

STEP 9

the following code could solve the database problem discussed above:

```
USE Mailings INDEX States
DO WHILE State = "CA"
  /*  Executable statements go here  */
  SKIP
ENDDO
```

The expression after the *DO WHILE* statement is the condition upon which the loop will continue to repeat. The statement *ENDDO* marks the end of the loop. Any statements in between consist of the body of the loop; they are the operations the loop will execute. In the example above, the loop will repeat as long as *State* contains the value "CA."

The USE Command

In this example, there are two Clipper commands you have not seen before. The first, *USE Mailings INDEX States,* is a command to establish which database (MAILINGS.DBF) and which index (STATES.NTX) to use. This command assumes that both of these files exist and are set up correctly. The *States* index is crucial—it orders the database by state; all the records with the same value for *State* will be contiguous. This is important because the loop ends when the first record that does not satisfy the condition is encountered. If the database is not indexed (or sorted) by state, it is possible that some records that do have *State* equal to "CA" will not be processed.

The SKIP Command

The other new command is SKIP. This simply tells the program to move the database pointer down one record, that is, to go to the next record before repeating the body of the loop.

You must have a statement in between the *DO WHILE* and *ENDDO* that alters the loop condition. If no such statement exists, your loop will execute forever—a programming error called an "infinite loop." If this occurs you can usually press the Ctrl-C key combination to quit your program. However, it is better to avoid such mistakes from the outset. Clipper's compiler and debugger will not catch this error.

EXIT and *LOOP*

Special situations will often occur in which you will want to get out of a loop before it ends. Clipper provides two commands to do this: *EXIT* and *LOOP*. *EXIT* will jump to the bottom and then pass out of the loop. Whatever statement immediately follows your *ENDDO* statement is then executed. *LOOP* will jump to the bottom of the loop as well, but instead of passing control out of the loop, it will then continue to the top of the loop, permitting the loop to continue.

DECISION-MAKING STRUCTURES

Whenever you want to execute program statements based on a condition, you can use either of Clipper's two decision-making structures: *IF...ENDIF* or *DO CASE...ENDCASE*.

IF...ENDIF Conditional Structures

IF...ENDIF is Clipper's more general conditional control structure and a basic element of every Clipper program. *IF...ENDIF* provides a flexible structure for evaluating conditions: it will execute a statement (or statements) if a condition is true, or it can execute alternative program code if the condition is false. The syntax is:

```
IF <condition1>
  <statements>
[ELSEIF <condition2>]
  <statements>
[ELSE]
  <statements>
ENDIF
```

Essentially, the IF structure will execute the code following the first true condition it encounters. Every false condition will cause a branching to the next ELSEIF or ELSE statements, or to the end of the structure if none remain. The expressions *<condition1>* and *<condition2>* *must* be logical expressions. If a condition is true, then all following statements are executed until an ELSEIF, ELSE, or ENDIF is encountered. The optional ELSEIF statement allows another condition to be specified, and its code will execute *only* if its condition is true *and* every previous IF and ELSEIF conditions were false. Any number of ELSEIF statements are allowed. Statements followed by ELSE (also optional) will execute only if all preceding IF and ELSEIF conditions were false. Every IF structure *must* end with an ENDIF statement. The absence of an ENDIF will generate an error during compilation. Here are some examples of *IF...ENDIF* structures:

```
LOCAL Users := 10
IF Users > 5
  ?"The Network is busy."
ELSE
  ?"The Network is not busy."
ENDIF
```

In the above example, different messages will be displayed on a computer screen depending on the numeric value of a variable.

```
IF EOF()
  ?"End of File Reached."
ELSEIF BOF()
  ?"Beginning of File Reached."
ELSE
  ?"The Current Customer is " + Cust_name
ENDIF
```

The BOF() and EOF() functions

This second example is slightly more complex. It uses the two Clipper database functions BOF() and EOF(). BOF() returns a value of .T. (true) if the database record pointer has reached the beginning of the database. EOF() returns a value of .T. if the pointer has reached the end of the database. (These two functions are very useful—you will see them many more times in this book.) So, this IF structure displays one message if the record pointer has reached the beginning of the database and another message if it has reached the end; if neither of these conditions is true, it displays the current customer.

The DO CASE Structure

Clipper offers another conditional control structure which is in fact identical to *IF...ELSEIF...ENDIF.* It is the *DO CASE...ENDCASE* structure. As a general rule, use the CASE structure whenever your software requires a conditional control structure that would use two or more ELSEIF conditions. For this kind of structure, *DO CASE...ENDCASE* is more readable than its *IF...ENDIF* counterparts. Its syntax is:

```
DO CASE
CASE <condition1>
  <statements>
[CASE <condition2>]
  <statements>
[OTHERWISE]
  <statements>
ENDCASE
```

The CASE structure will execute only the block of program code following *the CASE statement whose condition is true*. After that code is finished, the program will jump to the line immediately following the ENDCASE statement. Any number of CASE statements is allowed. The OTHERWISE statement is optional, and will execute its statements if none of the preceding CASE conditions are true. When the CASE structure reaches a true condition, all statements are executed until the next CASE, OTHERWISE, or ENDCASE statement is encountered. Any valid Clipper statements or control structures can be nested in a DO CASE structure.

CASE structure example

A common use of a DO CASE structure is to control branching from a menu. While menu structures will be discussed in detail in Step 11, it will be instructive to look at the DO CASE structure for the main menu of a program here. Assume that the user input from the menu was the variable *mChoice*.

```
DO CASE
CASE mChoice = 0 .OR. mChoice = 5
  CLEAR
  QUIT
```

```
CASE mChoice = 1
  Add_Cust()
CASE mChoice = 2
  Edit_Cust()
CASE mChoice = 3
  Reports()
CASE mChoice = 4
  Utilities()
ENDCASE
```

This case structure shows how the user of the program, by selecting the different choices on the menu, will perform different operations on his or her database. Each case option executes a different procedure (written by you) to do different actions.

The only choice that does not invoke a procedure is the first one; it executes two Clipper commands. The first is *CLEAR*. It erases the screen, then positions the cursor at the upper-left corner of the screen. You should always clear the screen upon terminating an application—otherwise your software will appear messy. The second command is *QUIT*, which closes any open database files, terminates the execution of the program, and returns the user to DOS.

So why are *CLEAR* and *QUIT* executed if *mChoice* is 0 *or* 5? The 5 corresponds to the selection of the last (fifth) menu choice, which presumably was to quit the program. However, this kind of menu (which will be explained fully in Step 11) will output a zero if the Esc key is pressed. This allows the user of the menu to exit the program in either of two ways: by selecting the last menu choice, or by pressing the Esc key. Of course, if you did not want to enable the Esc key for this menu, you could simply not include a case statement for *mChoice = 0*. You can see how the basic design of the application is reflected in this *DO CASE...ENDCASE* structure. These statements would be placed in the initial procedure of the application along with whatever setup and menu drawing commands were necessary. Each option in the menu (and therefore each case) calls a different procedure, or set of procedures. Thus, designing your programs with structures like this makes it much easier to write small, modular programs, the benefits of which I discussed earlier.

30

Procedures and Functions

The last three Steps have described progressively larger and larger pieces of Clipper programs. This Step is about the largest building blocks of programs: procedures and functions. Procedures and functions provide convenient ways to group sections of code, which can then be executed without your worrying about exactly how that code works. By breaking programming tasks into small sections, procedures and functions make your programs easier to write, test, and understand. Therefore, well written Clipper programs will tend to be collections of relatively short functions and procedures.

DEFINING PROCEDURES AND FUNCTIONS

Procedures and functions are very similar, although they are different enough to both be useful. The primary difference between the two is that functions *return a value* and procedures do not. The ramifications of this difference will be discussed throughout this Step. Arguments can be passed to both procedures and functions.

Defining Procedures

Procedures are little subprograms that perform a (hopefully) related set of Clipper commands. They can occur anywhere in a program

(.PRG) file, and do not return a value. The syntax for procedures is:

```
PROCEDURE <proc_name> [<parameter list>]
  <variable declarations>
  <executable statements>
[RETURN]
```

Every procedure must have a unique name. The parameter list is optional, and will be discussed in greater detail below. Note that variables must be declared before the executable statements begin. Although the *RETURN* statement is optional, I recommend that you use it anyway—it will make your code less confusing. If you do leave out the *RETURN,* the procedure will automatically come to an end and return to the calling procedure when the next *PROCEDURE* or *FUNCTION* statement or the end of the file is encountered. You have already seen some simple examples of procedures, such as *My_Proc*, in Step 7.

Defining Functions

Functions (also called user-defined functions) are very similar to procedures, except that they return a value. They take the following form:

```
FUNCTION <func_name> [<parameter list>]
  <variable declarations>
  <executable statements>
RETURN <return expression>
```

Function example

Since functions return a value, the *RETURN* statement is required. Of course, if the data returned from a function is incorrectly typed, a runtime error will occur. Here is an example of a function that returns the greater of two variables:

```
FUNCTION Greater( var1, var2 )
  LOCAL Greatest
  IF var1 > var2
    Greatest := var1
  ELSE
```

```
    Greatest := var2
  ENDIF
RETURN( Greatest )
```

One nice feature of *Greater()* is that, since Clipper variables can be of any type, variables of any data type can be input into this function.

Flexibility of return statements

An important feature of Clipper functions is the flexibility of the return statement in functions. *Greater()* returned a simple value, but return statements can include any legal Clipper value or expression. Since the return statement not only returns a value but also terminates processing of the function, you can have more than one return in a function, allowing conditional return-value processing. For example:

```
FUNCTION Check_Type( nVar )
  IF VALTYPE( nVar ) = "C"
    RETURN( "Character string " ;
      + RTRIM( nVar ) )
  ENDIF
RETURN("Not a character string.")
```

In this example, the function *Check_Type()* will return the expression in the third line if the passed parameter is of character-data type. If this condition is not true, the string at the end of the function will be returned. This function calls two Clipper functions. The first, VALTYPE(), returns a different character depending on the data type of the argument. In *Check_Type,* the only data type of interest is character, for which VALTYPE() returns "C." The other function, RTRIM(), removes trailing spaces from character strings.

CALLING PROCEDURES AND FUNCTIONS

Functions that you create are called in the same manner as Clipper functions. When you call a function, you must always include the open and close parentheses, whether or not you pass arguments to the function. Multiple arguments must be separated by commas. Here are some examples:

```
Cost := Greater( Cost1, Cost2 )
SETCOLOR("B/G, W+/N")
```

```
Zip_code := LEFT( q_zip, 5 ) + "-" ;
  + RIGHT( q_zip, 4 )
```

The first example shows how the function *Greater()* is used as an expression. It will return the greater value of the variables *Cost1* and *Cost2*. The second example shows how a function can be a statement all by itself. In this case, the Clipper function SETCOLOR() is used to change the colors of the screen. Finally, the two Clipper functions LEFT() and RIGHT() are used to build a zip code from a character string variable *q_zip*.

Calling procedures

Since procedures do not return values, they are usually specified in statements. A procedure is called simply by typing its name, as you would a Clipper command. However, there is one caveat: even if you are not passing any parameters to the procedure, you must still include the open and close parentheses after the procedure name. For example, the procedure *My_Proc* is called like this:

```
My_Proc()
```

Yes, it is that simple. If a procedure requires input, it is called like this:

```
Samp_proc( Samp1, Samp2, Samp3 )
```

In this case the procedure *Samp_proc* was invoked, and the three variables in its argument list were passed to it. As you can see, the syntax for calling procedures and functions is identical.

PARAMETERS AND ARGUMENTS

When you invoke a function or a procedure, you can pass values or references to it. In technical Clipper terminology, the values in the call to the function or procedure are called *arguments*. Thus, in the last example, *Samp1*, *Samp2*, and *Samp3* are called the arguments of the call to *Samp_proc*. The values on the receiving side are called *parameters;* for example, *var1* and *var2* in the function *Greater()* are parameters.

Skipping parameters

A few notes on parameters: Parameters that are defined as part of the function or procedure declaration, as in *Greater()*, act as local variables for that function. Also, the number of arguments does not have to match the number of parameters specified in the called procedure or function. Arguments can be left off the end of an argument list, or just skipped in the procedure call. For example, in the call to *Samp_proc,* if you didn't want to pass a value to the second parameter, you would type:

```
Samp_proc( Samp1,,Samp3 )
```

The absence of a value between the commas means that none was passed to *Samp_proc* for that parameter. Any parameter that is not received by an invoked procedure (or function) is given the value NIL.

Finally, remember that any variables that have been declared as PRIVATE in a procedure are accessible to any called procedures or functions, whether or not they are explicitly passed to that subroutine.

Passing Parameters by Value

The default manner in which values are passed to functions or procedures is by *value*. This means that the actual argument itself *is not* passed to the called subroutine. Instead, the program makes a copy of the value of the argument variable, and the called subroutine works with that copy. Thus, the called subroutine cannot change or affect the original variable in any way. This makes your subroutines independent of one another, and more modular. You have seen many examples of this kind of parameter passing above.

Passing Parameters by Reference

The other way in which parameters may be passed is by *reference.* This idea should be familiar to C programmers. When you pass a parameter by reference to a subroutine, you pass a reference (or pointer) to the memory location of the passing value instead of a copy of that value. This means that if the called routine changes the value of the parameter, the value of the original argument will be changed as well. A variable is passed by reference if the @ operator is placed before it in the function (or procedure) call. Look at the following example:

```
LOCAL Name := "Fred Flintstone"
LOCALnSuffix := "Jr."
Join_Name( @Name, nSuffix )
?Name
/*  Result:   Fred Flintstone, Jr.  */
PROCEDURE Join_Name( First, Add_on )
  If Add_on <> NIL
    First := First + ", " + Add_on
  Endif
RETURN
```

In this case, the procedure *Join_Name* takes two parameters. The variable names *First* and *Name* both refer to the same value, since *Name* was passed by reference. Thus, when *First* is redefined in *Join_Name,* the variable *Name* will also contain this new value. The *IF...ENDIF* statement in *Join_Name* ensures that there is a value to tack on to the end of the first parameter. If there is no value, the procedure does nothing.

Because passing values by references allows you to change the original variable, you should use this Clipper feature sparingly and carefully. In Clipper Summer '87 you could *only* pass variables by reference using the *DO...WITH* statement. Although Clipper 5.01 supports this statement, you should avoid using it so that you can use the preferred method of passing variables by value. I only mention it here for readers familiar with old versions of Clipper. If you are upgrading your programs to Clipper 5.01, you should change all *DO...WITH* statements to the new procedure- and function-calling syntax, passing variables by reference (with the @ operator) only when absolutely necessary.

MAIN PROCEDURE DEFINITION

The first lines of program code to execute when you start an application are those at the beginning of the first object file listed in the link command used to create the application. This is the only time in your application when program statements not enclosed in a procedure will be executed. For an example of such a program, see SAMPLE.PRG, which we created in Step 3. However, it is possible to enclose in a procedure a program's initial code.

This initial procedure is sometimes called a *main* procedure. To use a main procedure, you must do two things. First, when compiling the file that contains your main procedure, you must use the /N option. This tells the compiler that you will be defining a main procedure in this file. Second, make sure you place your initial procedure at the beginning of the first source file in the link object file list. If you follow these steps, Clipper will execute your main procedure first when starting up your application.

BEYOND THIS STEP

Although you cannot use nested procedures or functions, Clipper does support recursion. You are also allowed to pass arrays and code blocks as arguments to functions and procedures.

45

Programming with Menu Structures

Clipper's menus can make your applications both easy to understand and easy to use. The menus discussed in this chapter are *light-bar menus*—menus in which the current choice is highlighted. Light-bar menus are particularly appealing because a user can make choices with just the arrow and Enter keys.

The goal of this Step is to enable you to design a completely functional menu program that you can later modify to work with your own applications. In order to reach this goal, we will have to discuss a number of Clipper commands. A complete example of a menu program is given at the end of the Step.

USING THE @... COMMANDS

In previous Steps, some examples of Clipper code were given that used the Clipper Command *?* or *??* to display information to the screen. For tests and samples, *?* and *??* are sufficient, but in actual applications they are rarely used. Ultimately, *?* and *??* are too limiting; they do not allow you enough control over text placement on screen. Clipper does supply another set of commands, however, that provides precise control of where information is displayed. These commands all begin with the @ symbol.

The @...SAY command

The @ command that corresponds with the *?* and *??* is *@...SAY.* The basic syntax of this command is:

```
@ <row>, <column> SAY <expression>
```

The <row> and <column> values are numbers that correspond with coordinates on screen. The minimum value for row and column coordinates is zero. You can determine the row and column limits using the Clipper functions MAXROW() and MAXCOL(). For example, to display the date using the DATE() function in the upper-left corner of the screen, you might use:

```
@ 0, 0 say DATE()
```

The *@...SAY* command is quite flexible, and will be described in much greater detail in Step 15. It is introduced here to demonstrate the standard structure of @ commands. The @ sign is always followed by a set of screen coordinates, then the particular @ command, and additional arguments as necessary. Three @ commands (two cosmetic, one required) are particularly useful for setting up light-bar menus, and are discussed below.

@...CLEAR

This first @ command will clear a space on your screen, so you can be sure that your menu will not be cluttered with random junk from previous display commands. The syntax is:

```
@ <top>, <left> CLEAR TO <bottom>, <right>
```

The four coordinates define which portion of the screen will be cleared, as in the following example:

```
@ 0, 0 CLEAR TO 5, 80
```

This statement would clear a broad swatch at the top of your screen. Clearing space in which to work is but the first step in drawing menus, however.

@...TO

This @ command is also purely cosmetic, but will help to make your screens more readable, especially if many menus will be displayed on top of each other. *@...TO* draws a box on screen. It uses the syntax:

```
@ <top>, <left> TO <bottom>, <right> [DOUBLE]
```

Drawing a double-line box

Four coordinates are required for the *@...TO* command. Without the optional *DOUBLE* specified at the end of the statement, the *@...TO* command will draw a single-line box on screen. With *DOUBLE* specified, the command will draw a double-line box, as in the following example:

```
@ 5, 10 CLEAR TO 10, 40
@ 5, 10 TO 10, 40 DOUBLE
```

In this example, a space is cleared on the screen, and then a double-line box is drawn in that space. Note that if *<top>* and *<bottom>* are the same, a horizontal line will be drawn. If *<left>* and *<right>* are the same, a vertical line will be drawn. Once you have drawn your boxes, you can paint your screens inside them. How to do that is discussed next.

@...PROMPT

The one essential @ command for menus is *@...PROMPT.* This command paints a menu item at a specified screen location. The syntax for *@...PROMPT* is:

```
@ <row>, <column> PROMPT <menu item> ;
  [MESSAGE <message item>]
```

Creating onscreen menus

The *MESSAGE* option allows you to associate a message with each menu item. Messages are displayed at a preset screen location. Here is an example of the definition of a single menu choice:

```
@10,15 PROMPT "Utilities" ;
  MESSAGE "Access file manipulation utilities."
```

STEP 11

A complete menu is made up of a series of *@...PROMPT* commands, with the addition of one more command to make all these prompts do something. Read on!

USING MENU TO

Activating menus

Once you have defined your prompts, the menu is activated with the *MENU TO* command. Activation allows the application user to move among the menu choices with the arrow keys. Then, when the user makes his or her menu selection (by pressing Enter), *MENU TO* stores a value, based on the choice, into a variable. The syntax is:

```
MENU TO <menu variable>
```

If *<menu variable>* has not been defined, it will be created by *MENU TO* as a private variable. If *<menu variable>* has been defined and initialized, it determines which menu item is initially highlighted; otherwise, the first menu choice is highlighted. The value of *<menu variable>* returned by *MENU TO* is always numerical. If the first menu item was selected, *MENU TO* returns a 1, if the second, it returns a 2, etc. If the user presses Esc, a value of 0 is returned. See the following example:

```
@8,15 PROMPT "Data Maintenance" ;
  MESSAGE "Add, Modify, or Delete Records."
@10,15 PROMPT "Utilities" ;
  MESSAGE "Access file manipulation utilities."
MENU TO menu_choice
```

Menu_choice would be given a value of 1 if the user selected "Data Maintenance," 2 if he selected "Utilities," and 0 if he pressed Esc. A more detailed example will be shown at the end of this Step.

MENUING RELATED SET COMMANDS

Two Clipper SET commands are relevant to menu programming. They are *SET MESSAGE* and *SET WRAP.*

Using SET MESSAGE

Defining message location

You were probably wondering exactly how you decide where those menu messages will appear. You make your choice using the Clipper SET MESSAGE command. Its syntax is:

```
SET MESSAGE TO [ <row> [CENTER] ]
```

This command instructs messages to appear on the screen at row *<row>* and column 0. If you use the CENTER option, the messages will be centered on the screen, as in the example below:

```
SET MESSAGE TO MAXROW() CENTER
```

This command will center messages on the bottom row of any monitor. Note that *<row>* and CENTER are optional. You can specify the command as:

```
SET MESSAGE TO
```

This command will suppress the display of messages until another *SET MESSAGE* is encountered.

Using SET WRAP

SET WRAP allows you to decide whether or not your menus will wrap around, that is, move the current highlighted menu item from bottom to top and vice-versa with one press of an arrow key. Its syntax is:

```
SET WRAP on¦OFF
```

You can set wrapping either on or off. The Clipper default is menu wrapping off.

SAVING AND RESTORING SCREENS

Once you start displaying multiple menus and other information on the screen, you will notice that your computer monitor can get very crowded. You can eliminate this crowding by overlaying menus and screens on top of each other. But this solution causes another problem: how do you restore an old screenful of information once you are finished with a menu? Clipper lets you save and restore screens, so that you can overlay new menus and other information, then restore the old screen without losing anything. You do this with the SAVESCREEN() and RESTSCREEN() functions. The syntax for these are:

```
SAVESCREEN( <top>, <left>, <bot>, <right> )
```

and

```
RESTSCREEN( <top>, <left>, <bot>, <right>, ;
  <screen variable> )
```

With these two functions, you can save and restore any portion of the screen, and you can restore a saved section of a screen to a different place on the screen, as in the following example:

```
PROCEDURE S_Saver
  LOCAL cScreen, cColor
  cScreen = SAVESCREEN( 0, 0, MAXROW(), ;
    MAXCOL() )
  cColor = SETCOLOR()
  Menu_Proc
  SETCOLOR( cColor )
  RESTSCREEN( 0, 0, MAXROW(), MAXCOL(), ;
    cScreen )
RETURN
```

This procedure saves the entire screen to the variable *cScreen,* then executes the procedure *Menu_Proc.* After *Menu_Proc* is finished, the original screen (and its colors) is restored. Note that saving a screen does not change or clear the screen in any way; that is the domain of subsequent commands.

The SETCOLOR() function

In this example, the Clipper function SETCOLOR() is used twice. Before the call to *Menu_Proc,* the current color settings were saved in the variable *cColor.* Then after the subroutine is done, the SETCOLOR() function is used again to reset the system colors to those in effect before the procedure call. Thus, the values stored in *cColor* become the arguments of the SETCOLOR() function. By saving and varying color information like this, an application can be made more visually appealing. See the following program example for some additional *SETCOLOR()* examples.

THE PROGRAM EXAMPLE

Now that I have introduced all this information about menu creation, it is time for a detailed example. You should type the set of procedures and functions shown in Figure 11.1 into your computer so that you can experiment with the commands, as well as practice using the editor, compiler, and linker. This code can later become the seed from which your own software can grow.

```
/*  Sample Program Demonstrating Lightbar Menus  */
LOCAL mChoice, cScreen

CLEAR                                              //Clear the screen
SET WRAP ON

DO WHILE .T.
  mChoice := Do_Menu()             //Activate menus and get choice

  DO CASE                           //Case statements for the menu
  CASE mChoice = 0 .or. mChoice = 4           // Exit application
    CLEAR
    QUIT

  CASE mChoice = 1                                   //Add records
    cScreen := SAVESCREEN()
    /*  Place call to first procedure here  */
    Temp_Proc()
    RESTSCREEN(cScreen)

  CASE mChoice = 2                                       //Reports
    cScreen := SAVESCREEN()
    /*  Place call to second procedure here  */
    Temp_Proc()
    RESTSCREEN(cScreen)

  CASE mChoice = 3                                     //Utilities
    cScreen := SAVESCREEN()
    /*  Place call to third procedure here  */
    Temp_Proc()
    RESTSCREEN(cScreen)

  ENDCASE
ENDDO                                          //Main program loop
QUIT

/*  Function Do_Menu(): paints and activates main menu  */
FUNCTION Do_Menu()
  LOCAL cColor
```

■ ***Figure 11.1: The sample menu program***

```
  STATIC mSelection := 1
  SET MESSAGE TO MAXROW() CENTER

  /*  ISCOLOR() checks if the current monitor is color  */
  /*  Skip color operations for monochrome systems  */
  IF ISCOLOR()
    cColor := SETCOLOR()
    SETCOLOR( "gr+/b, w+/bg, n, n, w+/g" )
  ENDIF
  @ 6, 18 CLEAR TO 15, 59
  @ 6, 18 TO 15, 59 DOUBLE                          //Draw a box
  @ 8, 19 TO 8, 58                     //Draws a horizontal line

  /*  PADC() centers a character string  */
  @ 7, 19 SAY PADC( "Application Main Menu", 40 )
  @ 10, 24 PROMPT PADC( "Add Customers", 30 ) ;
    MESSAGE "Add new customers to the database."
  @ 11, 24 PROMPT PADC( "Print Reports", 30 ) ;
    MESSAGE "Print reports and labels."
  @ 12, 24 PROMPT PADC( "Utilities", 30 ) ;
    MESSAGE "Execute file utilities."
  @ 13, 24 PROMPT PADC( "Quit", 30 ) ;
    MESSAGE "Exit the application."
  MENU TO mSelection

  /*  Erase the Message Line  */
  @ MAXROW(),0 SAY SPACE( MAXCOL() )

  /*  If system is color, restore the old color settings  */
  IF ISCOLOR()
    SETCOLOR( cColor )
  ENDIF

RETURN( mSelection )      //Send value back to calling procedure
/*  Procedure to inform the user that a selected
    menu option is not yet available.  */
PROCEDURE Temp_Proc
  LOCAL tColor, tMenu

  SET MESSAGE TO                     //Turn PROMPT messaging off.
  IF ISCOLOR()
    tColor := SETCOLOR()
    SETCOLOR( "b/gr, w+/b, n, n, w+/g" )
  ENDIF

  @ 14, 37 TO 18, 74 DOUBLE
  @ 16, 38 TO 16,73
  @ 15,38 SAY ;
    PADC( "Selection Not Available", 36 )
  @ 17,38 PROMPT ;
    PADC( "Press Enter to Continue", 36 )
  MENU TO tMenu

  /*  Erase this display  */
  @ 14, 37 CLEAR TO 18,74

  IF ISCOLOR()
    SETCOLOR( tColor )
  ENDIF
RETURN
```

■ *Figure 11.1: The sample menu program (continued)*

To compile, link, and run this program, assuming that it is contained in the file MENU.PRG, type the following commands at your DOS prompt:

```
CLIPPER Menu
RTLINK FILE Menu
Menu
```

30

Database Concepts and Creation

Now that you understand the basics of programming with Clipper, you are probably wondering: What about databases? This Step (and the next two) detail everything you will need to know to create and manipulate databases in your applications. The main subject of this Step is the Clipper utility DBU.EXE, the tool with which you will initially set up your databases. DBU has some other useful abilities, and those will be discussed as well.

DESIGNING A DATABASE

Before actually creating the database, you must first design it. When you design the database (or databases) for an application, you must ask yourself three basic questions: What information will I need? How do I want to manipulate it? How should it be organized? As with designing a program, the more exactly you iron out the details before you begin, the fewer headaches you will have later.

What Information Is Needed?

I will demonstrate a simple database design by using an example: Let's say you want to create a database (and application) that can generate mailing labels for the customers of a music store. You want to be able to send advertising copy to these customers based upon the music they purchase. The information you will need is name, address, and recordings purchased. Does this mean that you will need one database with three fields? Definitely not!

How Will You Manipulate the Data?

Since you want to be able to sort the customers by last name, you will need separate fields for first and last name. And, since you will want to generate mailing labels for different locations, more than one address field will be required. You should split up the address into street address, city, state, and zip code.

Finally, there is the purchase data. Will one field do? You probably will need at least two: one for a name or description of the item, and the other for a coded inventory number. What if a customer buys more than one item? How about five pairs of fields? What then if he purchases more than five products? You can see the problem developing here. We require an unknown number of fields for potential purchases; implementing a large number (say fifty) would be difficult to work with. The solution? Create another database!

How Should the Data Be Organized?

Creating another database presents us with another problem. When writing our program, we will want to be able to coordinate data between the two databases; in other words, make sure that a customer in the first database is linked to his or her purchases in the second. This problem is solved by creating a common field (that is, a field with *exactly* the same name) in both databases. What should it be? We could use last name, but then what if two customers have the same last name? The same trouble could occur if we use both first and last name. What we need is a field that will contain a short, unique value for each customer. Let's just make one up! We'll call it *customer number,* or *custnum* for short.

Relational Databases

Our future application can assign a customer number to every person added to the database. Then, since the field *custnum* will be in both databases, we can create a link between the databases so that we can automatically get the purchase data for each customer. What we have created here are called *relational databases*: multiple databases able to access each other's data via a common field. Generally, you should use a new relational database whenever you need to keep track of many instances of the same kind of data. In the example above, we needed to keep track of multiple purchases, so we created a database just for purchases. We have arrived at our database design:

Database I	***Database II***
Customer Number	Customer Number
Last Name	Purchase Description
First Name	Product Number
Street Address	
City	
State	
Zip	

Now that we have designed our databases, it is time to actually create them.

DBU: CLIPPER'S DATABASE UTILITY

DBU is a complete database design environment that you run from your DOS prompt. DBU has many capabilities, including database, index and view creation, and browsing. In some ways it is similar to dBASE III+'s Assistant, or dBASE IV's Command Center, although it is far less functional than either of those environments. The next section will discuss DBU's essential tools.

INVOKING DBU

Starting DBU is as simple as typing DBU at your DOS prompt. If you followed the installation directions in Step 1, you should be able to run DBU from any directory on your computer. Start DBU now. The next several sections will lead you through all the steps necessary to create a database and then input data. As the key sequences for the rest of DBU's functions follow the same general patterns, they will only be discussed briefly.

CREATING A DATABASE USING DBU

The first screen that you see when starting DBU is split into two primary areas. Above the long line near the top of the screen is DBU's menu or menu bar. In the middle of the screen is what is called a *view*. Your view tells you what databases (with fields and indexes) are currently open. Up to six databases may be open at once. A few general rules for DBU: The Esc key will almost always exit you from the current operation. Pressing F1 and Enter provides onscreen help. Finally, DBU will often display messages and prompts (i.e., Yes or No questions) in the upper-left portion of the screen immediately below the menu bar. Get used to looking there.

The Menu Bar

The row of names and keys along the top of the screen comprise the menu bar. The menu bar is almost always available, and works in concert with most windows. To activate a menu, press the menu key associated with it; for example, press F1 for the Help menu. After you press the menu key, the associated menu will drop down, displaying all available options.

Using DBU's drop-down menus

The current menu choice will be highlighted. If no menu choices are highlighted, then none are currently available. The ↑ and ↓ keys change the highlighted choice as you would expect. The → and ← keys move you to adjacent menus. Pressing the Esc key will exit you from the current menu to the previous operation. You select the current highlighted menu choice by pressing Enter.

Now that you are in DBU, let's create a database. To create a new database, do the following:

1. Press F3.

Note that *Database* is highlighted. If you press ↑ or ↓, the highlighter does not move; *Database* is your only available option.

2. Press Enter.

Now a window appears with an empty structure. How to fill it in will be discussed next.

Windows

Field definition with DBU

DBU has many different windows, each associated with a particular menu command. They all have the same general feel, although the specifics of each window will depend on the task it is trying to accomplish. This particular window is the Structure window. It allows you to create or modify existing database field structures.

Note that every field must have a defined type and width. The allowable data types coincide with the primary variable types: character, date, logical, numeric, or memo. The width defines the maximum length of the field. For example, a state field would be of type character and of length two. Let's enter the field structure for this database:

1. Type **CUSTNUM**.
2. Press Enter twice.
3. Type **8**.
4. Press ↓.

These commands have defined the first field for your database. It has the name CUSTNUM, is of character type, and has a width of 8. If you wanted to select a different type, you would have pressed the Spacebar until the desired type appeared. If you pass your choice, just press the Spacebar five times and that value will come around again.

The last down arrow moved you to the next field. Now follow the same steps to enter the rest of the fields: FIRSTNAME Char 10, LASTNAME Char 15, ADDRESS Char 30, CITY Char 15, STATE Char 2, and ZIP Char 5. Yes, the zip code field should be character type data! Since you will not need to perform mathematical operations on zip code data, it will be easier to work with zip codes as character strings.

After the last field (for zip code) is entered, do not press ↓. If you already have, press once. You are now done. Your screen should resemble Figure 12.1. If you made any errors, you can move to the incorrect data with the arrow keys and correct your mistake. When you are satisfied with the structure, press F4, then Enter.

This sequence selects the *Struct* choice on the Save menu. You are about to save the database. To do so, you will have to successfully use the last major kind of window in DBU: the dialog box.

The Dialog Box

Whenever you need to perform an operation on files, you will be prompted with a dialog box. Dialog boxes contain *fields, buttons,* and *scrolling lists.* A field is a space that you have to fill in, perhaps with a file name. A button is a control that performs an action on the dialog box. Typically, dialog boxes contain *OK,* which saves your choices, performs the desired action, and closes the window; and *Cancel,* which closes the window without saving your choices.

Working with dialog boxes

You can move between the fields, buttons, and scrolling lists with the arrow keys. To fill in a field, you move the highlight to that field and begin typing, or move to the right and select a choice from the

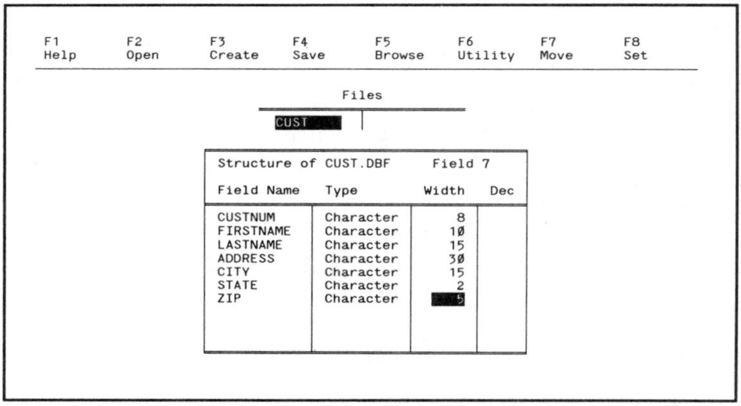

■ ***Figure 12.1: DBU's Database Structure Definition window***

scrolling list for that field. To select buttons or choices from scrolling lists, highlight them and press Enter.

You might remember that we were about to save the database you just created. You should be looking at your dialog box in DBU, having just pressed F4 and Enter.

1. Type **CUST** (this is the name of the database).
2. Press Enter.

Notice that you did not give the database a file extension. When you hit Enter, DBU automatically gave CUST the correct extension (.DBF). Also, note that OK is highlighted now. Your screen should look like Figure 12.2.

3. Press Enter.

You have successfully navigated the dialog box. Your database is saved and listed under *FILES* on your screen. The view shows you the currently open database in the first workspace with its fields listed below.

You now have used all the basic structures of DBU, and created a database to boot! Now let's do something else with DBU.

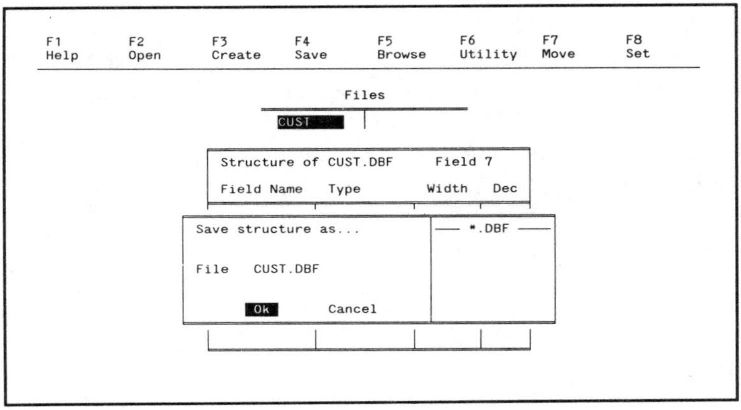

▪ ***Figure 12.2: A DBU dialog box***

STEP 12

CREATING AN INDEX WITH DBU

You are probably wondering how to create an index for CUST.DBF. It is quite easy. First, position the highlight on CUST in the view. If you haven't done anything since the last section, it should be there already. Then do the following:

1. Press F3
2. Press ↓ to highlight *Index* on the menu.
3. Press Enter. The Index creation window appears.
4. Type **CUST**. This will be the filename.
5. Press Enter. The extension .NTX is assigned to CUST.
6. Type **LASTNAME+FIRSTNAME**. We will discuss why below.
7. Press Enter. *OK* is highlighted.
8. Press Enter again.

Now you have created an index for CUST.DBF called CUST.NTX. The file will be indexed on the name of the customer. Since we used *LASTNAME+FIRSTNAME,* the database will be in alphabetical order by name, with duplicate customers with the same last name ordered by their first name.

Quitting DBU

Before you leave DBU, create another index based on just the field CUSTNUM. Then create a new database for purchases, as discussed earlier. Call it SALES.DBF. Both this index and database will be used in a later Step. When you are finished with this program, simply press the Esc key, answer Yes, and out to DOS you will go.

30

Basic Database Commands

In the last Step, you created your first database and index. In this Step (and the next), you will learn how to manipulate them with Clipper's database commands, while building on the ideas discussed in Steps 6 and 12. dBASE users are in luck—many of these commands will be familiar to you.

DATABASES AND WORK AREAS

Whenever you use a database in a Clipper application, you are required to define a unique place in which the database exists. That place is called a *work area.* Work areas are required so that you can manage more than one database without confusion. For example, you can use databases that have the same field names because all fields are referenced by their work area. Up to 250 work areas (and databases) may be open at a time. Each work area may contain a database, an associated memo file, and no more than 15 indexes. Work areas are defined with the USE and SELECT commands.

The USE Command

Working with one database

The basic command you will employ to open databases is *USE*. *USE* tells Clipper to open up the specified database in the current work area. After you execute the *USE* command, you can then perform actions on the database and its contents. The basic form of *USE* is

```
USE <database file> [ INDEX <index file list> ]
```

Where *<database file>* is the name of your database. The INDEX specification is optional; *<index file list>* is a list of one or more indexes (separated by comma). If more than one index is specified, all are open (up to 15) and the first one in the list is made active. For example, the *USE* command for CUST.DBF and CUST.NTX created in the last Step would be

```
USE CUST INDEX CUST
```

Assuming that you issued no previous USE or SELECT commands, CUST (and its index) would now be open in work area 1. It is not necessary to specify the extensions with this command; it will assume .DBF for databases and .NTX for indexes.

If your application only used this one database, you would need no additional USEs or SELECTs. Work area 1 would always remain open, and any database command would automatically affect the current database, that is, CUST.

Working with Multiple Databases and Work Areas

Work area numbers

If you wanted to work with more than one database, however, you would need to use slightly different commands. Before we get to those commands, we first need to discuss the two ways in which work areas are referenced. The first is by number. When you start up your program, Clipper will, by default, assume that the current work area is work area number 1 (as in the example above). When you have more than one work area, each is assigned a number (1, 2, 3, etc.). You can either define that number yourself, or you can have Clipper automatically open the next available work area.

Work area aliases

Additionally, each work area can be referenced by a special name called an *alias*. By default, the alias for a work area will be the same as the name of the database open in that area. However, it is possible to define your own alias names. It is often desirable to do this to make your program code easier to understand. Enough preparation, let's see some details!

The Advanced USE Commands

To use multiple databases, we will need a more complex form of *USE:*

```
USE <database file> ;
  [ INDEX <index file list> ] ;
  [ ALIAS <alias name> ] [ NEW ]
```

Two new options for USE are specified. One, ALIAS, allows you to specify an alias name for your work area. The other, NEW, is especially valuable. When you include it in a USE statement, it tells the system to open *<databasefile>* in the next available work area and make it the current work area. If you do not specify NEW, *<database file>* will be opened in the current work area. If there is already a database in the current work area, it will be closed to make room for the new one. To open the two databases CUST and SALES, you would use the following commands:

```
USE CUST
USE SALES NEW
```

This example opens the two databases (without indexes) in different work areas. Assuming that no other work areas were opened previously, CUST would be in work area 1 and SALES would be in work area 2. Without the NEW option, SALES would have been opened in work area 1 after CUST was closed. After these two commands were executed, work area 2 would be current, or active. Users of Clipper Summer '87 should note that the USE...NEW command supplants SELECT 0. This old method will still work, but is not preferred.

Using SELECT and SELECT()

Now that you have two work areas, each with its own database, how do you switch between them? Well, you use the SELECT command. It takes the form

```
SELECT <work area number> | <alias name>
```

You can select a work area using either its number or its alias. Thus, continuing with the previous example, you can use SELECT like this:

```
USE CUST
USE SALES NEW
SELECT 1
 //Code working with database CUST.
SELECT SALES
 //Code working with database SALES.
SELECT CUST
 //Back to CUST's work area.
```

Note that the work area number and alias can be used interchangeably. In this example, *SELECT CUST* and *SELECT 1* performed exactly the same operation.

How to find the current work area name

But what if you are using many databases, and are having trouble keeping track of which work areas are available, and which is current? Clipper supplies the SELECT() function with which you can retrieve the current work area name. In the following example, SELECT() is used to store the current work area name to a variable:

```
Old_area := SELECT()
USE Other_Database NEW
 //Program code for Other_Database here.
SELECT (Old_area)
```

The last line of this example uses the SELECT command to return to the previous work area. The variable *Old_area* is in parentheses to tell SELECT that the argument is stored in a memory variable, rather than as a simple number or alias name. The parentheses are required. Don't confuse this command with the SELECT() function.

Closing Databases

You can close databases and their associated files using either USE or CLOSE. By specifying USE alone on a line, you close the database in the current work area only. CLOSE by itself works the same way. However, you can close the databases in every work area by typing

CLOSE ALL. Finally, you can use CLOSE to close the files in a specified work area by using it as follows:

```
CLOSE <alias name>
```

Closing multiple databases

Finally, CLOSE and USE can be used with SELECT to close databases in more than one work area, as follows:

```
SELECT 1
CLOSE
SELECT 2
USE
SELECT Cust
CLOSE
```

RECORD SCOPING WITH DATABASE COMMANDS

Allowed scopes

Many commands can process subsets of records in a database with a scope and/or conditional clauses. A scope defines a set of records to be affected by the current command. The syntax for scopes and conditions is consistent for all the database commands that use them. Anytime a database command includes <*scope*> as part of its syntax, any of the following options are available: ALL, REST, NEXT (*number*), and RECORD (*number*). ALL instructs the command to operate on every record in the specified work area. REST processes all records from the current one to the end of the file. NEXT (*number*) processes the number of records specified, including the current record. For example, NEXT 10 would process the current record as well as the next 9. RECORD (*number*) processes only the single record specified.

Conditional clauses

Two different types of conditional clauses also may be specified. Each type of clause can use as its condition any allowable logical expression. A FOR clause checks *every* record in the work area, and performs the designated operation on those records that match the condition specified. A defined scope can limit the records that are processed with the FOR clause. A WHILE clause instructs the command to process every record in the defined scope (defaulting to REST if none is defined), except that it terminates when it reaches the *first* record for which the WHILE condition is false. Here is an example with the DELETE command:

```
DELETE NEXT 50 WHILE State = "OR"
```

This command will terminate after fifty records are processed, or after a record is reached whose value for the field variable *State* is not equal to "OR." Commands with record scoping will appear throughout this book.

ADDING DATA TO A DATABASE: METHODS AND IDEAS

Now that you can create databases and open them in work areas, you are probably wondering how to input data. While there are many ways data can be entered, only the most common techniques will be discussed here.

The Data-Entry Screen

The standard way to enter data into a database is to present the user with a screen with lots of blank spaces into which he or she can type data. Clipper gives you the freedom to design data-entry screens the way you want. How to design data-entry screens will be detailed at length in Step 15.

Using the Replace Command

Once you have your data collected (presumably stored in memory variables), you put it out to your database with the REPLACE command. The REPLACE command has the following syntax:

```
REPLACE <field> WITH <value> ;
  [,<field2> WITH <value2> ...] ;
  [ <scope> ] [ WHILE <condition> ] ;
  [ FOR <condition> ]
```

REPLACE can work with any number of fields at a time, and can be scoped absolutely and/or conditionally. Here is an example of the REPLACE command:

```
REPLACE Date WITH Order_Date + 1 ;
  NEXT Num_Items_Purchased
```

Using APPEND BLANK

Adding records to a database

There are two ways to add new records to a database. The first is *APPEND BLANK*. Its syntax is simply:

```
APPEND BLANK
```

This command adds one blank record to the end of the current active database, and moves the record pointer to that new record. The fields in that record are initialized to the default empty values for their particular data types.

ORDERING AND SEARCHING FOR DATA

Indexing and sorting were discussed in Step 6. Because of its speed advantage over sorting, only indexing will be discussed here.

Creating Indexes

It is possible to create every index for a database using DBU; however, you may want to create indexes within an application. You do this using the INDEX command. The index command will create an index for the current active database. Its syntax is

```
INDEX ON <index key> TO <index filename>
```

Open and active indexes

Generally, *<index key>* must be an expression involving fields in the current active work area. In its simplest form, the key will just be a single field. The *<index filename>* is the name of the file that will contain the new index. It is automatically given the extension .NTX. No more than 15 indexes may be opened in a single work area. If more than one index is created, all remain open (up to 15) and the last one is active, as in the following example:

```
USE Cust New
INDEX ON Zip to Zip
INDEX ON Lastname + Firstname TO Custname
```

The first example creates an index called ZIP.NTX that indexes the database on zip codes. The second index, CUSTNAME.NTX, indexes the database on the last name *and* the first name fields. With this index, all records that have the same last name will also be in alphabetical order by first name. Since CUSTNAME.NTX was created last, it would be the active index (although ZIP.NTX would remain open).

Using SET ORDER

Why is there all this fussing over open and active indexes? The reason is that all open indexes will be updated as the database is changed. Thus, if a new record is added, all open indexes will be modified to include the new record. This is very important, because if you try to use a database with an index that has not been kept up to date, you will probably see some very odd behavior. It is imperative that you keep all your indexes up to date. The simplest way to do this is to make sure that when you open your database (with USE) you specify every index that is associated with that database. This might result in a USE command like the following:

```
USE Cust INDEX Custname, Date, Zip, State
```

How do you work with all those indexes? You use the SET ORDER command. This command allows you to pick which of your open indexes will be active. Its syntax is

```
SET ORDER TO <index number>
```

The index number is based on the index list in the USE command for that work area. For the above example, the index Custname is index number 1, Date is 2, Zip is 3, etc. Thus, when you want to change the active index to zip code, you type:

```
SET ORDER TO 3
```

SET ORDER TO 0 or just *SET ORDER TO* without an argument deactivates any active index and restores the database to record number order, while still leaving all indexes open.

Searching with SEEK

All this time I have been telling you that indexes make searching much faster. To search with an active index, you use the SEEK command. Its syntax is

```
SEEK <search expression>
```

SEEK's only constraint is that it will only try to match the *<search expression>* with the field with which the current index was created. Thus, using the Cust database and its Custname index, you could do the following search:

```
SEEK "Smith"
```

The record pointer would move to the next record in which the LASTNAME field contains the string "Smith." If no such record were found, the record pointer would be moved to the end of the file.

BEYOND THIS STEP

There are a number of more advanced commands associated with those discussed in this Step. CLOSE has a number of other uses. It is possible to append records from another database using APPEND FROM. The COPY command allows you to copy records from the current database. Finally, the REINDEX, SET INDEX, and SET SOFTSEEK commands, as well as the DESCEND(), INDEXKEY(), and INDEXORD() functions, can be useful in some situations.

More Database Commands

This Step continues the discussion of the essentials of database manipulation. The topics in this Step include record deletion, filtering, database navigation, and establishing relations between databases.

DELETING RECORDS: A TWO-STEP PROCESS

One remnant from the dBASE language found in Clipper is the requirement to perform two separate actions to remove records from a database. These two steps provide a safety net—an opportunity to change your mind before *really* deleting data.

DELETE

Marking records for deletion

The first step in record deletion is the DELETE command. Contrary to its name, it does not actually delete a record; it merely *marks* records for deletion. Its syntax is

```
DELETE [<scope>] ;
  [WHILE <condition>] [FOR <condition>]
```

The full range of scoping options allows for great flexibility. The DELETE command used alone will mark only the current record for deletion.

Removing Records with PACK

When you are ready to remove deleted records from a database, you use the PACK command. It will remove all marked records from the current active database, and update all open index files associated with the packed database. Its syntax is

```
PACK
```

Packing a very large database can be a very slow process, so it is probably not an action that you will want to allow if speed is critical.

Undeleting Records

If, before packing, you should decide that you do not want to delete a particular record, you can unmark it for deletion with the RECALL command. Its syntax is

```
RECALL [<scope>] ;
  [WHILE <condition>] [FOR <condition>]
```

Removing Records with ZAP

If you need to remove all the records in the current database, as well as delete any associated index or memo files, you can use the *ZAP* command. Its syntax is

```
ZAP
```

ZAP essentially performs the same operations as DELETE ALL followed by PACK except that it is nearly instantaneous. However, it must be used with great caution: once you ZAP your database, it is gone forever!

DATABASE NAVIGATION

Moving the record pointer

There are often times when you will want to move the record pointer (change the current record) without performing any other actions. Clipper provides a number of commands to do this kind of operation. The simplest, SKIP, was discussed in Step 9. Its syntax is

```
SKIP <number of records>
```

The <*number of records*> can be either positive or negative, and tells the system how many records to move the record pointer. SKIP without an argument will jump to the next record. Note that SKIP will follow index order if any index is active.

Using GOTO

GOTO allows you to move the record pointer to either a specific record or to the top or bottom of a database. Its syntax is

```
GOTO <record number> ¦   BOTTOM ¦    TOP
```

Note that one of <*record number*>, BOTTOM, or TOP *must* be specified.

BOF() and EOF()

In a number of previous steps, the functions BOF() and EOF() were discussed. They are useful in determining location in a database. BOF() returns .T. at the beginning of a database, while EOF() returns .T. at the end of one.

FILTERING RECORDS

Filtering was introduced way back in Step 6. You might remember that a filter establishes a rule by which only a subset of the records in a database are visible to processing. Filters are activated with the SET FILTER command:

```
SET FILTER TO <logical condition>
```

Using filters

Once the filter is set, the work area functions as if only the records that match the *<logical condition>* exist. Most commands that move the record pointer will honor the filter, except those that access records by record number. Filters have no effect on indexes. Remember, the entire database still exists, so filtering will not make processing of the filtered records any faster than processing of the entire database. To turn the current filter condition off, use SET FILTER TO without an argument. Here is an example that filters a database to residents of New York:

```
USE Cust INDEX Cust NEW
SET FILTER TO State = "NY"
  //Perform processing.
SET FILTER TO                  //Deactivate filter.
```

The DBFILTER() function

The function DBFILTER() returns the current filter condition as a character string.

SETTING RELATIONS BETWEEN DATABASES

As was discussed in the last two Steps, Clipper allows you to use more than one database in an application, as well as establish links, or relations, between databases. Only one command and one operator are required to perform complex tasks involving many databases.

The -> Alias Identifier Operator

If you are using more than one database (and work area), you will often want to make explicit references to fields. This way, you can refer to fields in different work areas without changing the current work area with SELECT. You can explicitly state that a field is associated with a particular work area by using that work area's alias and the -> operator, as in the following example:

```
USE CUST          //Opens CUST.DBF in work area 1
USE SALES NEW
  //Opens SALES.DBF in work area 2
```

STEP 14

```
SELECT CUST
  //Selects work area 1 with alias CUST
Cust_tot := SALES->Price * SALES->Num_items
/*  Calculate a customer's total sales from
  the price and number-of-items-sold data
  from the SALES work area.  */
Sales_End := SALES->( EOF() )
/*  Check if the end of SALES.DBF has
  been reached.  */
```

This example demonstrates two uses of the alias identifier operator: to refer to a field in another work area, and to get information from a database in a different work area. But this example raises an important question: How do we know that the record from SALES contained information about the current customer in CUST? Unless the data in SALES was very limited, we couldn't. What we need to be able to do is establish a link or a relation between the two databases.

Using SET RELATION

Of course, Clipper provides for such relations, as was discussed in Step 12. To establish a relation between databases, you use the *SET RELATION* command, whose syntax is

```
SET RELATION TO ;
  [ <key expression> INTO <alias> ] ;
  [, <key expression 2> INTO <alias 2> ... ] ;
  [ ADDITIVE ]
```

Parent and child work areas

The current work area when the relation is set is called the *parent*. All work areas that the parent is linked to are called *child work areas*. Any parent work area may be related to no more than eight children. Note that each relation requires both a *<key expression>* and an *<alias>*. The *<alias>* is simply the identifier for the child.

Key expressions

The *<key expression>* is a field that both parent and child have *exactly* in common, and upon which the child is actively indexed. When a relation is set, every time the record pointer moves in the parent a SEEK is performed upon each child to find the corresponding record.

Setting multiple relations

The ADDITIVE option allows you to add relations to a work area. Without ADDITIVE, new SET RELATION commands will release any existing relations in the current work area before establishing the new ones. Here is an example:

```
USE Cust INDEX Cust NEW
  //Set up Work area 1
USE Sales INDEX Custnum NEW
  //Set up Work area 2
SELECT Cust
  //Select Work area 1
SET RELATION TO Custnum INTO Sales
  //Establish Relation
Cust_tot := Sales->Price * Sales->Num_items
```

In this example, both databases must have a field called CUSTNUM, and the active index for Sales (Custnum), must be keyed on that field. Now Cust_tot will definitely be calculated from the values in SALES.DBF that correspond to the current customer in the Cust database. You could set an additional relation from Cust into another database like this:

```
USE Mailings INDEX M_cust NEW  //new work area
SELECT Cust
SET RELATION TO Custnum INTO Mailings ADDITIVE
```

When no matching record is found

If no matching record is found in a child database, then EOF() is .T. for that database. Also, the function FOUND() would return .F. This function is set every time a SEEK is performed.

Screen I/O

Another standard element of any Clipper application is screen output. We have already discussed screen designs relating to menus, but another screen design awaits: the data-entry screen. A data-entry screen provides application users with a way to review the data in their databases, as well as to add new data. A flexible data-entry screen can perform both jobs.

THE AESTHETICS OF DATA-ENTRY SCREENS

Your data-entry screens, while probably not works of art, can possess a functional beauty. The aesthetics of data-entry screens are simple: They should be efficiently organized, easy to use, and most importantly, not too crowded. If you have too much data for one screen, do not cram it all on—find a coherent system for dividing the data into two groups and two screens.

THE BASIC DATA-ENTRY FORMAT

While Clipper provides a variety of quite complex data-entry methods, it is possible to design a usable data-entry system using a small

STEP 15

subset of those commands. For many applications, this kind of data-entry system is all you will need. The basic command of this system, @...GET, is like the @...SAY command discussed in Step 11, with a number of options added on. Its syntax is

The @... GET command

```
@ <row>, <col>
  [ SAY <expression> [ PICTURE <pict format> ] ]
  GET <variable>
    [ PICTURE <pict format> ] ;
      [ VALID <postcondition> ]
```

The SAY portion of this command is optional. Here is an example of an @...GET statement with a PICTURE, specifying that the input data must consist of five numerical digits:

```
@ 5, 10 GET Zip_Code PICTURE "99999"
```

The VALID option

The GET option VALID allows you to define a condition that must be true before you can proceed. While a simple logical expression could be used for the VALID condition, more complex statements are possible. In the example at the end of this Step, the return value from a function is used as the VALID condition.

Controlling How Data Is Displayed with PICTUREs

Controlling your data's display format is crucial. As in the above example, the PICTURE option allows you to define the way data input into a GET statement must look. It is possible to format an entire PICTURE with a single command (with a *function string*), or one character at a time (with a *template string*).

PICTURE function strings

Either or both kinds of strings can be present in a single PICTURE; if both are present, the function must precede the template, and the two must be separated by one space. All PICTURE formatting must be contained between double quotes. Function strings come first in PICTUREs, and are prefaced by the @ character. These are the most important function strings:

A Allows only alphabetic characters.

K Deletes default text if the first key pressed is not a cursor key.

! Converts alphabetic characters to uppercase.

PICTURE template strings

Template strings specify formatting rules for individual characters in a GET operation. These are the most useful:

A Allows only alphabetic characters.

X Allows any character.

9 Allows only digits.

Y Allows only Y or N.

L Allows only T, F, Y, or N.

! Converts alphabetic characters to uppercase.

Here are some examples of the use of function and template strings:

```
@ 5, 5 GET Area_Code PICTURE "@K 999"

@ 6, 5 GET Street_Address ;
  PICTURE "@! XXXXXXXXXXXXXXXXXXXX"

@ 7, 5 GET Sex PICTURE "@! A" ;
  VALID Sex = "M"  .OR. Sex = "F"
```

In the first example, the *@K* causes text in the field to be deleted automatically when you begin typing. The *999* allows only numbers to be entered. In the second example, the *Xs* allow any characters to be entered while the @! function capitalizes alphabetic data. Typing out twenty *Xs* in this PICTURE restricts the number of characters entered into this field to no more than twenty, no matter how many more characters the field may have. In the third example, only alphabetic data is allowed, and it will be instantly capitalized.

STEP 15

Full-screen input mode

GETs and READs

So what exactly does a GET do? Whenever the user encounters a series of @...GET statements, he or she is put into full-screen input mode. Data can be entered into any of the GETs, and the cursor keys can be used to move back and forth among the various data fields. Groups of GET commands are combined with a READ—generally you place one after a series of @...GET statements. READ says, "Make all the above GETs active for data entry in full-screen mode, until the last field is completed." Carefully examine the GET and READ combinations in the example at the end of this Step. Note how the Esc key is used to quit full-screen edit mode—this is the standard way to abort a READ without saving data.

Buffering Data

You can protect the data in your databases by using buffering. This is simply inputting data from GETs into memory variables instead of field variables, and then using REPLACE to store the memory variables' data into the database. Data buffering is important because it allows a GET-READ to be abandoned without changing the database. If data were input directly into field variables, escaping out of full-screen edit mode could cause unwanted data to get into the database. This technique is also demonstrated in the upcoming example.

A DATA-ENTRY PROGRAMMING EXAMPLE

The following long programming example should be combined with the example from the end of Step 11. Simply change *Temp_Proc()* to *Add_cust()* in the *mChoice = 1* CASE. Then enter the following example into a file (call it ADD.PRG). These are the DOS commands required to build and execute your new load:

```
CLIPPER Menu /M
CLIPPER Add
RTLINK FILE Menu, Add
Menu
```

You may need to compile ADD.PRG a number of times until you have typed in the program exactly as it appears here. Look out for typos! Type in ADD.PRG as it appears in Figure 15.1.

```
/*  Sample File Demonstrating Data Entry Screens  */
PROCEDURE Add_cust

LOCAL Confirm, Add_more := .T.
PRIVATE aCust, aLast, aFirst, aAdd, ;
  aCity, aState, aZip                          //Data Input Buffers

USE Cust INDEX Custnum NEW                      //Set up work area

/*  Clear and Box the area for the Menu  */
@24,0 CLEAR
@6,10 CLEAR TO 18,70
@6,10 TO 18,70 DOUBLE                                  //Draw a Box
@8,11 TO 8,69                                //Draw a single line
@7,11 SAY PADC("Customer Data Entry Window",59)

Paint_screen()                    //Screen initialization procedure

DO WHILE Add_more                 //Loop until finished adding data
  @19,0 SAY PADC( ;
    "ESC to quit without saving data", MAXCOL() )
  SET ESCAPE ON                     /*  Allows the user to escape in
                                              case of error.  */

/*  Buffer the input data.  */
  @10,24 GET aCust PICTURE "@! XXXXXXXX" ;
    VALID No_dupes(aCust)

  @ 12,24 GET aFirst PICTURE "@K !!!!!!!!!!"
  @ 12,51 GET aLast PICTURE "@K !!!!!!!!!!!!!!!"
  @ 14,24 GET aAdd ;
    PICTURE "@K! XXXXXXXXXXXXXXXXXXXXXXXXXXXX"
  @ 16,24 GET aCity PICTURE "@K! XXXXXXXXXXXXXXX"
  @ 16,48 GET aState PICTURE "@K !!"
  @ 16,62 GET aZip PICTURE "@K 99999"
  READ

/*  Don't save the data if the user pressed Escape  */
  IF LASTKEY() <> 27
    SET ESCAPE OFF

/*  Add and fill a new record in CUST.DBF  */
    APPEND BLANK
    REPLACE Custnum WITH aCust, Lastname WITH aLast, ;
      Firstname WITH aFirst, Address WITH aAdd, ;
      City WITH aCity, State WITH aState, Zip WITH aZip

  ENDIF

/*  Ask the user if he wants to add another record  */
  Confirm := 'N'
  @19,0 SAY PADC("Add another customer (Y/N)? ", ;
    MAXCOL() )
```

■ ***Figure 15.1: The data-entry screen example***

```
  @19,53 GET Confirm PICTURE "Y"       //Only "Y" or "N" allowed
  READ

  IF UPPER(Confirm) = 'Y'
    @19,0 CLEAR
    Paint_screen()                          //Refresh the screen
  ELSE
    Add_more := .F.                        //Quit adding records
  ENDIF
ENDDO                                //End of record adding loop

CLEAR                                      //Clean up the screen
USE                                       //Release the work area
RETURN


/*  No_dupes() checks for duplicate customer numbers.  */
FUNCTION No_dupes (cnum_check)
IF cnum_check = SPACE(8)                  //Blank customer number
  TONE(349,3)
  TONE(300,5)
  @10,34 SAY " Blank Customer # Not Allowed."
  RETURN .F.
ENDIF

GO TOP
SEEK cnum_check
IF .NOT. EOF()                //Duplicate customer number found!
  TONE(349,3)
  @10,34 SAY " Duplicate Number.  Try Again."
  RETURN .F.
ELSE                                 //Customer number not found.
  @10,34 SAY "                              "
  RETURN .T.
ENDIF
/*  No additional RETURN needed for this function  */


PROCEDURE Paint_screen
/*  Initialize the buffer variables  */
aCust := SPACE(8)
aFirst := SPACE(10)
aLast := SPACE(15)
aAdd := SPACE(30)
aCity := SPACE(15)
aState := SPACE(2)
aZip := SPACE(5)

/*  Paint the screen  */
@ 10,13 SAY "Customer #:"
@ 12,14 SAY "Firstname:"
@ 12,42 SAY "Lastname:"
@ 14,16 SAY "Address:"
@ 16,19 SAY "City:"
@ 16,42 SAY "State:"
@ 16,53 SAY "Zip Code:"

RETURN
```

■ ***Figure 15.1: The data-entry screen example (continued)***

BEYOND THIS STEP

A complete discussion of the Clipper GET system would require at least three or four times as much space as this Step allows. For hours of Clipper contemplation, see the GET class, Clipper objects, code blocks, and the functions GETNEW() and READMODAL() in your Clipper documentation. You may have noticed the function LASTKEY() in this Step's long example. It is only part of Clipper's keyboard system; for more information, see INKEY(), CHR(), NEXTKEY(), the SET KEY and SET TYPEAHEAD commands, and the INKEY.CH header file in your documentation.

30

Using RL to Create Labels

Most database applications require printed output. As usual, Clipper provides you with many options for printing, from the simple to the arcane. This Step describes the Clipper utility RL.EXE. RL is really two programs in one: a report writer and a label writer. RL emulates the dBASE III+ report and label creation commands, and even creates report (.FRM) and label (.LBL) definition files compatible with dBASE III+.

While RL is extremely useful for creating mailing labels, its report creation abilities are rather limited. I can only imagine using RL to design reports if I were very short of time, in need of an extremely simple columnar report, and unconcerned with the appearance of the report. Such situations rarely arise, however, so I recommend writing custom reports, which are discussed in the next Step. If you do need to use RL to create a report, be careful. RL can act unpredictably, especially with its F2 (Report) and F10 (Exit) menu choices.

However, if your application requires mailing labels, using RL is by far the quickest and easiest way to create mailing label definitions. This Step will show you how to create mailing label definitions with RL, then use those definitions in your programs.

RL BASICS

RL leads you through label (and report) creation using a series of windows and dialog boxes very similar to those you saw in DBU.EXE back in Step 12. You start RL.EXE by typing RL at your DOS prompt. As in other Clipper utilities, most operations in RL can be aborted by pressing the Esc key.

Go ahead and start RL now:

1. At your DOS prompt, type **RL**. The initial screen, while not inspiring, is uncomplicated. It allows you three options: Report, Label, and Quit.
2. To select your option, use the arrow keys to highlight the desired choice and press Enter.
3. Since we are going to design a mailing label, highlight Label by pressing → once; then press Enter.

CREATING AND MODIFYING LABELS

A dialog box very much like those in DBU should have appeared on your screen. At this point, you can create a label by entering a new file name. RL will add the extension .LBL to all label files. To modify an old label, you could either type the name of an existing label file or select one from the pick list at the right of the dialog box. The pick list should be empty now. To create the file, do the following:

1. Type **CUS_LBL**.
2. Press Enter. OK will be highlighted.
3. Press Enter again.

After the second Enter, RL will display the Label Editor screen (shown in Figure 16.1). When you enter the label editor, the top half of the screen (dimensions and formatting) is active.

The Label Utility menu

Along the top of the Label Utility screen are four menu choices, each of which is activated by pressing the function key associated with it. The current work file is displayed in the upper right. To create a label,

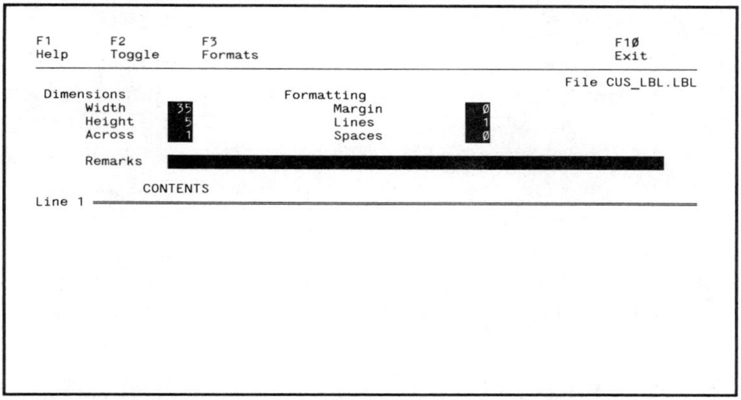

■ ***Figure 16.1: The Label Editor screen***

you must perform two steps: Define the label's dimensions and format and define the label's contents.

Defining a Label's Dimension and Format

The size of a label, as well as how it will be printed, is defined in the top half of the Label Editor screen, with the following attributes (see Figure 16.1):

Dimensions of a label

Width	The horizontal width of a label.
Height	The number of lines in a label.
Across	The number of labels printed across the page.
Margin	The first print position of the left labels.
Lines	The number of vertical lines between labels.
Spaces	The number of horizontal spaces between labels.
Remarks	A comment field.

You can move among the dimension and formatting attributes with the arrow keys. However, it may be difficult to determine how to format different kinds of labels. Instead of guessing, you can use one of RL's five standard label formats.

Choosing Standard Label Formats

To select a standard label format, simply press the F3 (Formats) key. The Standard Label screen should appear as shown in Figure 16.2. You can select one of the five standard labels by moving the highlight to your choice with the arrow keys and then pressing Enter. You can quit this window at any time by pressing Esc. To select standard *3 1/2 x 15/16 by 3* labels, press ↓ twice, then Enter.

The dimensions and formatting attributes have been modified to correspond to the standard label format that you selected.

Defining Label Contents

Once the format of your label is finished, you will need to define its contents. To access the contents portion of the Label Editor, press F2 (Toggle). This key toggles you back and forth between the contents and formatting sections. The contents section contains as many lines as were defined in the height dimension above. At the far left, the current line is displayed; it should now say *Line 1*. Let's fill this label with data from the database CUST.DBF.

1. Type **RTRIM(FIRSTNAME) + " " + LASTNAME.**
2. Press Enter.

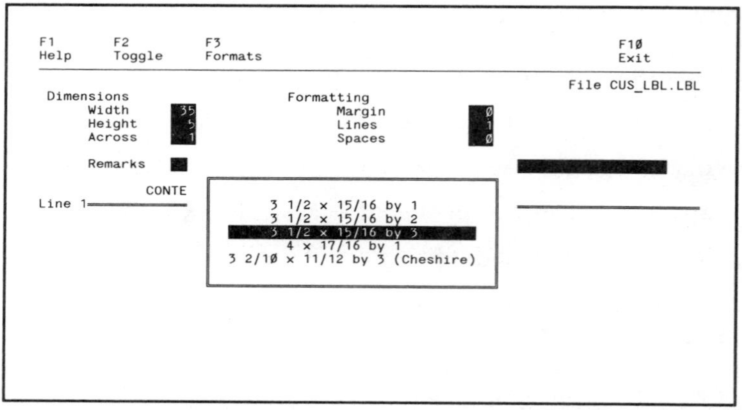

▪ *Figure 16.2: The Standard Label screen*

3. Type **RTRIM(ADDRESS)**.
4. Press Enter.
5. Type **RTRIM(CITY) + ", " + STATE + " "+ ZIP**.

Your screen should now resemble Figure 16.3. Remember that you toggle back to dimension and formatting by pressing F2. If you make an error or want to edit any field, highlight that field, press Enter, and then use → or ← to move to the desired editing position.

Be careful! If you start typing in a field without pressing Enter first, the entire contents of that field will be erased before the new information is entered. Try editing a few fields to get the hang of the system.

Saving Label Definitions

Once you are finished with your label definition, you can save it by pressing F10 (Exit). You will be presented with a very simple window that allows you three choices: *OK,* which saves changes made to the label and returns you to the Main menu; *No,* which discards any changes and returns you to the Main menu; and *Cancel,* which returns you to the Label Editor so you can continue working on your label definition. Once you have highlighted your choice, press Enter. In

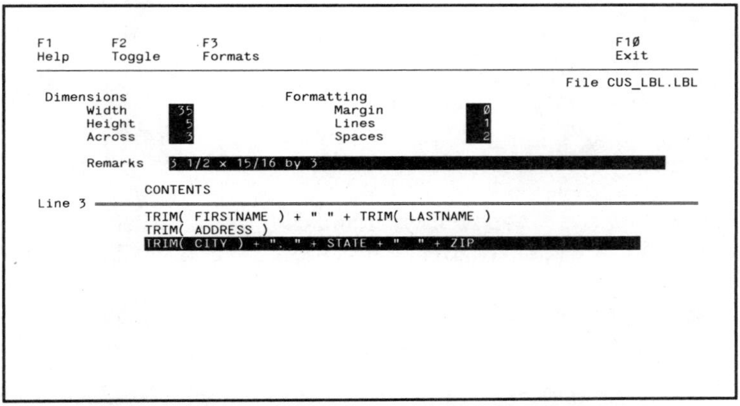

▪ ***Figure 16.3: The Label Editor screen with contents added***

this case, since OK should be highlighted, just press Enter to save and quit. Now you should be back in RL's Main menu.

QUITTING RL

You can exit RL by selecting Quit or pressing the Esc key while in the Main menu.

PROGRAMMING WITH RL'S LABELS

Once you have created a label definition file, you can use it to print labels in a program with a single command: LABEL FORM. Its syntax is

```
LABEL FORM <report name> ;
  [ TO PRINTER ] [ TO FILE <filename> ] ;
  [ <scope> ] [ WHILE <condition> ] ;
  [ FOR <condition> ]
```

This command will always send labels to your computer's screen (for the exception, see below). You can select options to send the data to either a printer or a file. Note that this command allows the full range of scoping; without any defined scope, a label will be printed for every record in the active database. Here is an example using the label definition created above:

```
/*  Sample Printing Program: Customer Number
  Order  */
USE Cust INDEX Custnum NEW
LABEL FORM Cus_lbl TO PRINTER
QUIT
```

This example is a complete program. The first line defines from which database (CUST.DBF, in this case) to access label data. The index Custnum defines the order in which the labels print. If you wanted to print out the labels in a different order, you could either use a different index or create one, as in the following example:

```
/*  Another Sample Printing Program: Zip Code
Order  */
```

```
USE Cust NEW
INDEX ON Zip TO ZIPS // Create a new Index
LABEL FORM CUS_LBL TO PRINTER
QUIT
```

Remember that the last index created with INDEX ON will remain active. You can compile, link, and run either one of these examples; they are both complete programs. When you run them, make sure that CUST.DBF, CUS_LBL.LBL, and any required indexes are in the current file directory.

Using SET CONSOLE

Controlling label output destination

Seeing label output on screen can be useful during application testing, but will probably become unnecessary. To turn it off, you use the SET CONSOLE command. Its form is

```
SET CONSOLE  off ¦ ON
```

When you set this command to OFF, no commands (except @...SAY's) will display to the console. To ensure that the console is turned off only during printing, use this command immediately before and after LABEL FORM, as shown here:

```
SET CONSOLE OFF
LABEL FORM Sales TO PRINTER
SET CONSOLE ON
```

THE PROGRAM BEHIND THE PROGRAM

Like many of Clipper's utilities, RL.EXE is actually written with Clipper. RL's .PRG files (RLFRONT.PRG, RLBACK.PRG, and RLDIALOG.PRG) are stored in the \CLIPPER5\SOURCE\RL directory. These files are provided so that you can examine and/or modify RL as you see fit. A make file (see Step 4), RL.RMK, is provided to allow easy recompiling and linking.

STEP 16

BEYOND THIS STEP

If you are having trouble aligning your printed labels, the SAMPLE option of LABEL FORM might be useful. Additional Clipper commands to control output to your screen or printer are discussed in the next Step. If you decide to use an existing dBASE III+ report definition, or create reports with RL, the Clipper command for printing .FRM files is REPORT FORM.

15

Writing Custom Reports

In the last Step, I told you not to use RL to create reports. Not only are RL's report creation abilities very limited, but by creating reports with RL you give up the flexibility that makes Clipper so valuable. If you write your own reports as Clipper programs, you can have complete control over the appearance, output, etc. of your reports. Paying clients will expect to see slick printed output, and with Clipper you can create it. If you have worked through the previous Steps in this book, you already know most of the programming tools required to write your own reports. This Step will discuss the remaining Clipper commands required. The next Step gives a detailed example. Remember—if you don't like my reports, you can use Clipper to create your own.

USING THE @ COMMANDS FOR PRINTING

Steps 11 and 15 introduced the @...SAY command. This command will be used just as it was for screen output, except that the column and row coordinates in your @ commands will now refer to positions for data on the printed page. By using @...SAY's PICTURE commands, as well as Clipper's text formatting functions (like RTRIM(), UPPER(), etc.), you can control the appearance of your printed output.

STEP 17

A few additional programming precautions must be taken when directing Clipper output to a printer. Since many printers compose and print a line at a time, it is important to organize your output so that you do not try to print data on a line that has already been completed. Typically, a counter is used to keep track of line numbers. After all the text on one line is printed, the counter is incremented. When the counter reaches a number that corresponds to the end of the page (there are about sixty lines on an 11-inch page), you can send a page eject command to the printer, reset the counter, and continue printing. In the example in the next Step, the variable *Line_num* is used to keep track of line numbers.

CONTROLLING PROGRAM OUTPUT

There are a number of Clipper commands that allow you to control where your output goes (i.e., to the screen or the printer) and to send control commands directly to a printer.

SET CONSOLE, SET PRINTER, and SET DEVICE

SET CONSOLE

These three SET commands must be discussed together because they have similar effects. SET CONSOLE was discussed in the last Step; it only enables/disables output to the screen. Other commands must be used to direct output to a printer or a file. Note that SET CONSOLE does not affect full-screen commands like @...SAY; their destination is controlled with the next command.

SET DEVICE

SET DEVICE only controls the direction of @...SAY commands. Its syntax is

```
SET DEVICE TO SCREEN | printer
```

If you create reports with @...SAYs, you *must* use this command to direct your output correctly. The other SET commands have no control over the destination of @...SAYs.

This last set command has two syntaxes. The first is

```
SET PRINTER on | OFF
```

Turning SET PRINTER on will echo all data displayed to the screen (except @...SAYs) to the printer. Its other form is

```
SET PRINTER TO <destination name>
```

The *<destination name>* can be either a file or a logical device like LPT1, COM1, etc., thus allowing you to control printing in an environment with multiple printers or to send data to a file. Note that @...SAYs will be sent to the destination set with SET PRINTER TO only if SET DEVICE TO PRINTER is active.

Remember that many Clipper commands (like LABEL FORM) have their own TO PRINTER or TO FILE options that can be used instead of these SET commands. The variety of SET commands relating to output direction may seem confusing at first, but be patient. They are designed to allow you the maximum control possible over output in your application environment.

The EJECT Command

You can send page ejects to your printer with the Clipper command EJECT. Its syntax is simply:

```
EJECT
```

In technical terms, this command tells the printer to advance the print head to the top of the next form.

Sending Control Commands to Printers

You can send control commands to your printer using the ?? command if SET PRINTER ON has been specified before beginning output. I have used such commands quite often with Hewlett-Packard laser printers. Look at the following example:

```
?? CHR(027) + '&l1O'
```

This command directs the laser printer to print in landscape mode. Printer control codes vary, depending on the printer; see your printer manual for its control codes. With control codes, you can direct your printer to use whatever type-faces, point sizes, etc. are available, thus allowing you further control over your printed output.

PRINTING WITH FILTERS AND INDEXES

Output directed to a printer will always obey any active filters and/or indexes. You can use this to your advantage to print out only a subset of the records in a database (with a filter) or to determine the order of printing (with an index).

ESCAPE ROUTES AND ERROR DETECTION

Since printing involves using a device that might be shared with other users and applications, your program should approach printing with care. You should always provide the user with at least one opportunity to change his or her mind before actually sending the job off to print. Then, you should provide a mid-processing abort or escape route, and not keep it secret—you should display on the screen how the user can quit the print job. For example, you might display at the bottom of the screen, *Press Escape to Abort Print Job*. Clipper provides many ways to create such escape routes, one of which will be discussed next.

On Canceling Print Jobs

The INKEY() function

It is quite common to give an application user the option to quit a print job before it is complete. This can be done using the INKEY() function. This function allows you to monitor what key (if any) has been pressed on the keyboard. It works like this: Every time a key is pressed, a value (one for each key) is stored in a buffer. INKEY() *extracts* the next key in the keyboard buffer and returns a numerical value identifying which key was pressed. INKEY()'s optional argument specifies the amount of time (in seconds) that the computer should wait for a key press. INKEY(0) will wait indefinitely until the user presses a key. A typical example is

```
LABEL FORM OLD_CUST TO PRINTER ;
  WHILE INKEY() != 27
```

This command will print labels using the active database and label definition OLD_CUST.LBL until the user presses the Esc key—its INKEY() return value is 27. INKEY() (as well as the Clipper functions NEXTKEY() and LASTKEY()) can be used to process keyboard input in many other situations as well.

Error Detection with Printing

Common problems, like not having the printer turned on or set on line, can cause your application to crash or behave oddly if printing is attempted. You could give your application user a chance to check his or her printer set-up before sending off the print job with the following commands:

```
@ 10, 40 CLEAR TO 16, 65
@ 10,40 TO 16,65 DOUBLE
@ 12,41 SAY PADC( "Check Printer Set-Up", 24 )
@ 14,41 PROMPT PADC( "Enter to Continue", 24 )
MENU TO CHECK_PRINT
```

The ISPRINTER() function

However, Clipper provides a function called ISPRINTER() that can check whether your printer is ready. This function only works with the LPT1: parallel printer port. It returns a true (.T.) if a ready printer is detected at that port; otherwise, it returns a false (.F.). Thus, you could use it as follows:

```
LOCAL Done_Printing :=  .F.
DO WHILE !Done_Printing
   @ 17, 20 SAY "Press Escape to Abort."
   IF ISPRINTER() // Print if Printer is online
      @ 15, 20 SAY "Printing . . .     "
      @ 16, 20 CLEAR TO 16, 50
      LABEL FORM Tax_Cust TO PRINTER WHILE
INKEY() != 27
```

```
      Done_Printing :=   .T.
   ELSE        // Tell user printer is not ready
      @ 15, 20 SAY "Printer Not Ready."
      @ 16, 20 SAY ;
           "Press a Key to Re-Try Printer."
      IF INKEY(0) = 27
           // If the user pressed Escape
         EXIT // Exit the loop
      ENDIF
   ENDIF
ENDDO
```

In general, the more you check for errors and allow for escape routes, the more foolproof your software will be.

BEYOND THIS STEP

Step 18 is a companion to this one. In it you will find a detailed example of custom reporting software using the commands, functions, and techniques discussed in this Step.

60

A Custom Report Example

This Step uses the Clipper programming techniques discussed in Step 17 to create a fully functional custom report. It can be interfaced with the menuing program created in Step 11 and modified in Step 15.

INTERFACING WITH THE MENU PROGRAM

To get your menu program to call this procedure is very simple. Change the procedure call in the third CASE (mChoice = 2) to read *CREPORT()* and recompile your menu program with the CLIPPER Menu command.

A FEW NOTES ON THE SAMPLE APPLICATION

Using the Databases

This application uses the two databases CUST.DBF and SALES.DBF as they were designed in Step 12. I have added a field called PRICE (numerical data, width 6, 2 digits after the decimal) to SALES.DBF. Add that field to SALES.DBF to practice your DBU skills. If you wish to test this program, you will need to enter data into CUST.DBF with ADD.PRG. You will also need to enter data into SALES.DBF. This can be done by creating a program that works with MENU.PRG and ADD.PRG, or by entering the data in the Browse mode of DBU.

New Clipper functions

To ensure that they are up to date, both required indexes are created in the example. The first, SALES_CN.NTX, keyed on customer numbers in SALES.DBF, is necessary because of the relation between the databases. The other, STATE.NTX, determines the records' print order. You might want to move index creation to MENU.PRG so that this (somewhat slow) process does not have to be repeated for every report that is generated. This example uses a few new Clipper functions. TRANSFORM() allows you to change any data type to a string and control its print formatting. REPLICATE() repeats a character the number of times specified. It is useful for drawing lines on reports. Finally, LASTREC() returns the total number of records in the current database.

CREATING THE NEW APPLICATION

Carefully type the example shown in Figure 18.1 into your computer. Call the file REP.PRG; if you call it CREPORT.PRG, your compiler will confuse the file and procedure names. Once you have finished your typing, you can compile the program with the DOS command CLIPPER REP. You may need to compile and correct the file a few times to eliminate typing errors. After you have successfully compiled the program, you can link the menu, customer addition procedure (from Step 15), and report program with:

```
RTLINK FILE Menu, Add, Rep
```

Run the application by entering its name in DOS: Menu.

```
PROCEDURE CREPORT                        //Prints Customer Purchase Info.

LOCAL Line_num, Do_Print := ' ', Num := 1, Page := 1
LOCAL Cust_Tot_Sales, Num_recs, Recs := 0, Tot_Sales := 0
PRIVATE Page_position

IF ISCOLOR()                                  //Check for Color Monitor.
  SET COLOR TO W+/R                        //Reset color for this window.
ENDIF

@  8, 20 CLEAR TO 14, 70
@  8, 20 TO 14,    DOUBLE&a1728H70                         //Draw Window.
@ 11, 21 SAY PADC( "Send Data to [P]rinter or [Q]uit?", 48 )
```

■ *Figure 18.1: The sample program*

```
/*  Allow the user to Quit the program without printing.  */
@ 11, 62 GET Do_Print PICTURE '!' ;
  VALID Do_Print $ 'PQ'
READ
IF Do_Print = 'Q'              //Quit Procedure if Quit Selected.
  @  8, 20 CLEAR TO 14, 70
  RETURN
ENDIF

@ 11, 21 CLEAR TO 11, 69                   //Erase the Query Line.
@ 12, 21 SAY PADC( "Press Escape to Abort Printing", 48 )

USE Sales NEW
INDEX ON Custnum To Sales_CN             //Index Sales on custnum.
USE Cust NEW                                      //Open Cust.DBF.
SET RELATION TO Custnum INTO Sales
Num_recs := LASTREC()                 //How many records in the db?

/*  Now create a new index for Cust based on State and Name. */
INDEX ON State + Lastname + Firstname TO State

/*  This variable defines where the page number will print.  */
Page_position := MAXCOL() - 8

SET DEVICE TO PRINT                   //Send output to the printer.
GOTO TOP                         //Go to the start of the database.
/*  Print every record or until Escape is pressed.  */
DO WHILE .NOT. EOF() .AND. NEXTKEY() != 27

/*  Print the header at the top of each page.
    Line_num is passed by address because it
    is updated in Print_Header.  */
    Print_Header( @Line_num, Page )

/*  Print the Data until end of file or page is reached, or
    if the user presses Escape.  */
  DO WHILE .NOT. EOF() ;
    .AND. Line_num < 55 ;
    .AND. NEXTKEY() != 27

/*  Update the user on the progress of the print job.  */
    SET DEVICE TO SCREEN
    @ 10, 21 SAY PADC( "Printing # " + ;
      TRANSFORM( ++Recs, "@B 99,999" ) + " Out of "  + ;
      TRANSFORM( Num_recs, "@B 99,999" ) + " Records", 48 )
    SET DEVICE TO PRINT

/*  Only calculate the total sales for a customer if
    he/she has a customer number (custnum).  Since
    sales data is referenced by custnum, a customer
    without one must have no sales.  This bit of error
    checking prevents the system from getting confused
    by looking for sales data for a customer who has none.  */

    IF Custnum <> SPACE(8)
      Cust_Tot_Sales := Cust_Sales()
    ELSE
      Cust_Tot_Sales := 0
    ENDIF
    Tot_Sales := Tot_Sales + Cust_Tot_Sales
```

Figure 18.1: The sample program (continued)

```
/*  Print the current customer's data.  */
    @ Line_num,  2 SAY SUBSTR( STR( Num ), 8, 3 ) + '.'
    @ Line_num,  8 SAY RTRIM( Lastname ) + ', ' + ;
      RTRIM( Firstname )
    @ Line_num, 38 SAY City
    @ Line_num, 58 SAY State
    @ Line_num, 65 SAY Cust_Tot_Sales
    Num = Num + 1
    Line_num = Line_num + 1
    SKIP                       //Go to the next customer's record.
  ENDDO
  IF .NOT. EOF()
    Page := Page + 1
    EJECT
  ENDIF
ENDDO

IF INKEY() = 27                          //If job was aborted . . .
  SET DEVICE TO SCREEN
  @ 10, 21 SAY PADC( "Printing Aborted at Record # " ;
    + TRANSFORM( Recs, "@B 99,999" ), 48 )
  @ 12, 21 SAY PADC( "Press any key to continue", 48 )
INKEY(0)                //Halt operations until a key is pressed.
ELSE                                /*  Print out sales totals.  */
  Print_Total( @Line_num, @Page, Tot_Sales)
ENDIF

SET DEVICE TO SCREEN
@  8, 20 CLEAR TO 14, 70
CLOSE ALL
RETURN

/*  Procedure to print sales totals.  */
PROCEDURE Print_Total( tLine, tPage, tTot )
  IF tLine > 50                              //End of form reached?
    EJECT
    tPage = tPage + 1
    Print_header( @tLine, tPage )
    tLine = tLine + 5
  ELSE
    tLine = tLine + 2
    @ tLine, 2 SAY REPLICATE( "-", 76 )
    tLine = tLine + 2
  ENDIF

  @tLine, 2  SAY "TOTAL SALES"
  @tLine, 65 SAY tTot
  EJECT
RETURN

/*  This function returns a customer's total sales.  */
FUNCTION Cust_Sales()
LOCAL Cur_custnum, Total := 0
  SELECT Sales                     //Select the Sales work space.
    //Price and Custnum are fields in SALES.DBF.
  Cur_custnum := Custnum

/*  Add up the sales in the current customer's records.  */
  DO WHILE Custnum = Cur_custnum
    Total := Total + Price
```

■ *Figure 18.1: The sample program (continued)*

```
    SKIP
  ENDDO

  SELECT Cust                     //Return to the Cust work space.
RETURN Total

/*  This procedure prints the Header for each Page.  */
PROCEDURE Print_Header( hLine, hPage )
  hLine := 0
  @ hLine, 3  SAY 'DATE: ' + DTOC( DATE() )
  @ hLine, Page_position ;
    SAY 'PAGE: ' + ALLTRIM( STR( hPage ) )
  hLine = hLine + 1
  @ hLine, 0 SAY PADC( "Example's Record Store", MAXCOL() )
  hLine = hLine + 1
  @ hLine, 0 SAY PADC( "State/Sales Report", MAXCOL() )
  hLine = hLine + 2
  @ hLine,  2 SAY 'No.'
  @ hLine,  8 SAY 'Name'
  @ hLine, 38 SAY 'City'
  @ hLine, 57 SAY 'State'
  @ hLine, 67 SAY 'Total Sales'
  hLine = hLine + 1
  @ hLine, 2 SAY REPLICATE( "=", 76 )
  hLine = hLine + 1
RETURN
```

■ *Figure 18.1: The sample program (continued)*

45

Debugging with CLD

Clipper comes with one more utility that needs to be discussed: CLD, the Clipper debugger. A debugger is a program that allows you to view your application's code and data as it is running. CLD is especially useful because it is designed with debugging database applications in mind; not only can you use it to view your source code and the values of variables and expressions, but you can get information on what databases are in use, as well as what indexes, filters, relations, etc. are active. While the version 5.0 and 5.01 CLDs are very similar, this step will discuss only the details of the version 5.01 CLD.

WHY USE A DEBUGGER?

Why would you care to look at your code as it is running? If you have never used a debugger before, the answer is far from obvious. Debuggers help you test your software (find "bugs") by allowing you to examine its processes in action. In a short program this might not be so useful, but in a long program many subtle problems can arise. What do you do when you are sure you wrote the code correctly, but it does not work? With CLD, you can observe the code as it is running, and carefully check variables and operations until you spot the error. Then you fix the procedure, compile, link, and continue testing.

PREPARING TO USE CLD

In order to use the Clipper debugger, you must compile every program file in your load with the /B option. This option tells the compiler to include debugging information in object files. You can save a lot of time if you are using a make file: simply change the compile instruction in that file, erase all your object files, and remake your application. Thus, your inference rule might look something like:

```
.PRG.OBJ:
  Clipper C:\CLIPPER5\SOURCE\MUSIC\$* /B
```

Including path information in the inference rule tells CLD where to find your program file. This is necessary only if you are going to debug your application in a directory different from that in which its .PRG files are stored.

Do not use the /L (compile without line numbers) option. CLD cannot provide information about applications compiled in this manner.

Before you distribute your fully tested code, you may want to recompile all the program files with the /L option and without /B (and then relink). Applications compiled without debugger information and line numbers will be significantly (usually about 20 percent) smaller.

INVOKING THE CLIPPER DEBUGGER

To debug your software with CLD, enter at your DOS prompt:

```
CLD <executable file>
```

For example, to debug the application that has been developed in Steps 11, 15, and 18, you would type:

```
CLD Menu
```

Try it now. When you issue this command, the program will begin and your computer screen will look like Figure 19.1.

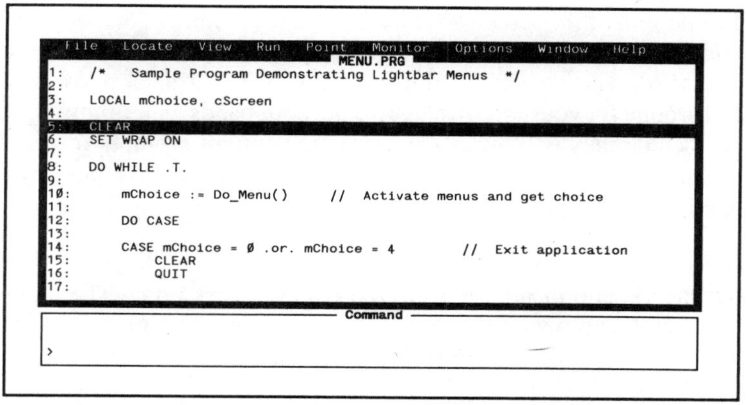
File Locate View Run Point Monitor Options Window Help
MENU.PRG
1: /* Sample Program Demonstrating Lightbar Menus */
2:
3: LOCAL mChoice, cScreen
4:
5: CLEAR
6: SET WRAP ON
7:
8: DO WHILE .T.
9:
10: mChoice := Do_Menu() // Activate menus and get choice
11:
12: DO CASE
13:
14: CASE mChoice = 0 .or. mChoice = 4 // Exit application
15: CLEAR
16: QUIT
17:
Command
>

▪ *Figure 19.1: The debugger screen at program initiation*

DEBUGGER BASICS: A WEALTH OF CHOICES

As with many of Clipper's tools, there is always more than one way to do something in CLD. In fact, CLD provides three primary ways to control your debugging session: with function keys, with menus, and with direct commands. Each of the control modes will be discussed, with a typical debugging session (of MENU.EXE) used for examples. Your screen should still resemble Figure 19.1.

Windows

The code window

The CLD screen includes a number of windows, each containing unique information. Right now, you can see two windows, the *code window* and the *command window.* The code window displays your program's source code. The highlighted line is the line of code about to execute. Since the Menu program has just begun, the highlighted line is *CLEAR.* You might also notice a flashing cursor. This is called the *position indicator.* While it begins on the same line as the highlight bar, it can be moved independently of that bar without executing program code. To move the position indicator, use ↑ and ↓. Try that now.

The command window

The bottom of the screen always displays the command window. In this window, you can enter CLD commands, a number of which will be discussed in this Step. The greater-than sign (>) in this window acts as a prompt for your commands. To enter commands, you simply type characters; they will always appear at the current prompt. You can also use → and ←, as well as the Backspace, Del, and Ins mode keys to edit your commands.

The Go command

Let's try a common command now. To get your program started, you use the Go command. So now type **Go** and press Enter. The main menu of your program should now appear. Your program is running, and if you do not wish to use the debugger, you could execute it normally.

Returning to the Debugger

To return to CLD during program execution, press the Alt-D key combination. Try it now. Your screen should now look like Figure 19.2. Note that the information in the code window is different from that in Figure 19.1. A number of lines of code have been executed, and the current line (about to execute) is farther along in the software. The current highlighted line should read *MENU TO mSELECTION*.

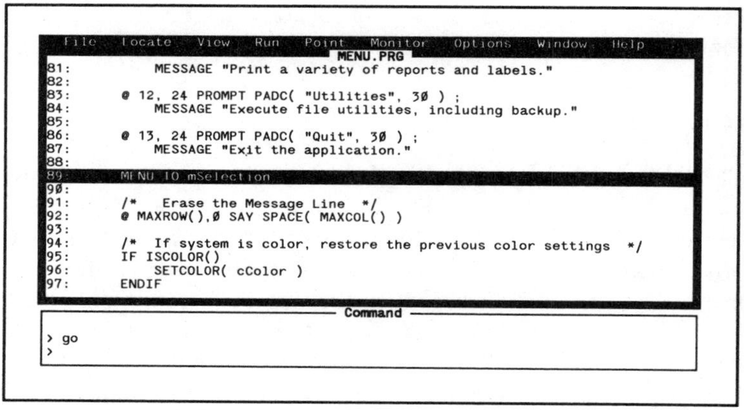
File Locate View Run Point Monitor Options Window Help
MENU.PRG
81: MESSAGE "Print a variety of reports and labels."
82:
83: @ 12, 24 PROMPT PADC("Utilities", 30) ;
84: MESSAGE "Execute file utilities, including backup."
85:
86: @ 13, 24 PROMPT PADC("Quit", 30) ;
87: MESSAGE "Exit the application."
88:
89: MENU TO mSelection
90:
91: /* Erase the Message Line */
92: @ MAXROW(),0 SAY SPACE(MAXCOL())
93:
94: /* If system is color, restore the previous color settings */
95: IF ISCOLOR()
96: SETCOLOR(cColor)
97: ENDIF
Command
> go
>

■ *Figure 19.2: The debugger screen after the first Go command*

Using Function Keys

You already have seen how to enter a CLD command. While there are many more (about 30), it is also possible to control your debugging session with function keys. Nearly all of the function keys have command equivalents, but their ease of use makes them invaluable tools. The most important function key is F8, the Step key. Pressing this key once will execute the current line of code. Press F8 now. Your Main menu should have reappeared. Remember that your program is not in a continuous run mode; the menu has appeared because the current line of code (*MENU TO mSELECTION*) requires input.

The first menu choice, *Maintain Customers,* should be highlighted. Select that choice by pressing Enter. Now you are back in the debugger. The Step key has allowed the execution of a single line of code. Press the F8 key eight times (more if you if have a color monitor). As you do this, you can follow the operation of your program as it uses the input to mSelection to decide which procedure to execute. In this case, Add_Cust() is selected, and as you press the Step key you will see the debugger jump to that procedure (i.e., the code window will contain the beginning of Add_Cust()).

You can examine the rest of the function keys on your own. Of particular use are F1, the Help key, which will display information about the commands and function keys; and F4, which displays the current screen that the application user would see. To leave either the help or application screens, press Esc.

Using CLD's Menus

The last way to control CLD is with its menus. While the menus duplicate many of the commands or function keys, they provide easy access to much information. To view a menu, press the Alt key in combination with the first letter of the desired menu. We are going to look at the *Monitor* menu: Press Alt-M. You can move among the menus by pressing → or ←; menu choices can be selected with ↑, ↓, and the Enter key. The Monitor menu has five choices. Each (except the fifth) displays a different class of variables on the screen. Let's select Local variables. To do this, press ↓ three times and then press Enter.

Your screen should now look like Figure 19.3. This menu command opens a new window called the *monitor window.* This is an important window; it displays variables and their values. You can often find bugs by carefully observing the values of variables as your application executes. If you wish to place or delete a specific variable (or expression), instead of an entire class, you use the Point menu watchpoint command. This creates another window, the *watch window,* which displays valves of user-selected variables.

Working with Multiple Windows

If you wish to observe more variables than will fit in the watch or monitor windows, you use ↑ or ↓ to scroll the contents of the window. However, since these keys will also provide scrolling in the code window, you must be able to select which window is active. CLD makes this quite simple: Press the Tab key until the window you wish to use is displayed surrounded by a thick line; that window is the active one. Thus, you can switch among the watch, monitor, and code windows, scrolling in each as necessary.

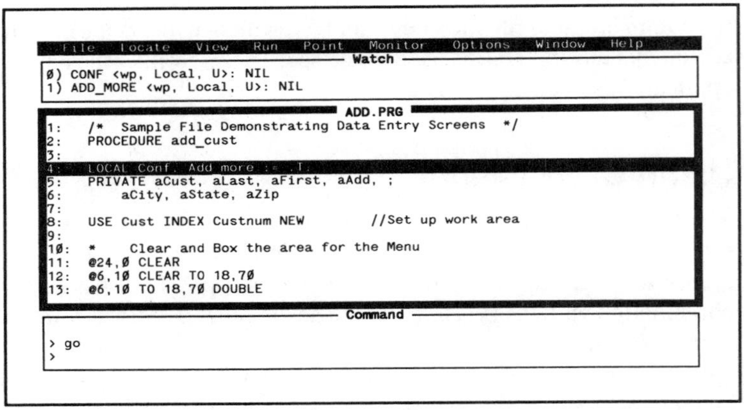

File Locate View Run Point Monitor Options Window Help
Watch
Ø) CONF <wp, Local, U>: NIL
1) ADD_MORE <wp, Local, U>: NIL
ADD.PRG
1: /* Sample File Demonstrating Data Entry Screens */
2: PROCEDURE add_cust
3:
4: LOCAL Conf, Add more := .T.
5: PRIVATE aCust, aLast, aFirst, aAdd, ;
6: aCity, aState, aZip
7:
8: USE Cust INDEX Custnum NEW //Set up work area
9:
1Ø: * Clear and Box the area for the Menu
11: @24,Ø CLEAR
12: @6,1Ø CLEAR TO 18,7Ø
13: @6,1Ø TO 18,7Ø DOUBLE
Command
> go
>

■ *Figure 19.3: The debugger screen with a watch window*

Breakpoints

The last important CLD feature I will discuss is the *breakpoint*. A breakpoint is a specified line of code at which the application will halt execution. Breakpoints are particularly useful because they allow you to run a program only up to a certain line of code about which you might have some doubt. To set a breakpoint, move the position indicator to the line of code at which you want the application to stop, then press F9 (pressing it again turns the breakpoint off). Let's try setting a breakpoint. At this point, your screen should still resemble Figure 19.3.

1. Press the Tab key until the code window is active.
2. Move the position indicator (with the ↓ key) to line 22 of the current program (it should be ADD.PRG).
3. Now press F9.

You can now type **Go** in the command window, and the program will execute until line 22 is reached, at which point execution will halt, CLD will start, and you will see line 22 highlighted. When you debug your own software, you will find breakpoints very useful to control program flow.

QUITTING CLD

There are three ways to quit CLD. You can type **Quit** in the command window, select Exit from the File menu, or press Alt-X. Note that when you quit the application that is running under CLD, you are returned to the debugger, not to DOS. This gives you the choice of either restarting the application (or another) or quitting CLD.

BEYOND THIS STEP

While the concepts and techniques discussed in this Step can certainly start you on the path of successful software debugging, we've only scratched the surface of CLD here. Remember, the debugger is a tool designed to make your life easier, not harder.

30

Networking

Any database application developed with Clipper will work on a local area network (or LAN). However, unless special networking commands are employed, Clipper will not allow access to files and records by more than one user. Therefore, if your application requires the sharing of database information, you must design your program appropriately. This Step introduces the production of shared database applications with Clipper.

LAN REQUIREMENTS

Any network on which you wish to run a Clipper application must adhere to DOS 3.1 or later function calls. Also, every workstation on the network must be running under DOS 3.1 or later. DOS 3.1 or a more recent version is required because Clipper uses this DOS standard for all its network-related system calls. If you are unsure whether your network is compatible with DOS, consult your network operating manual or dealer.

NETWORKING BASICS

There are three main issues that must be considered when designing a networking application: file sharing and locking, record sharing and locking, and data visibility.

STEP 20

On File Sharing

Generally, you will want to be able to share a database file among users so that they can all access its information simultaneously. However, there will be certain circumstances under which you will wish to lock a file, that is, only allow one user to access or update a file. This is the most restrictive sharing or locking decision you can make.

When to lock files

You will need to lock a file whenever you perform a command that writes data to more than one record in a file, such as DELETE, RECALL, or REPLACE. If you attempt any of these commands on multiple records without first locking the relevant database files, Clipper will generate an error. File locking is required in these cases to ensure data integrity—to avoid writing data to a file when another user is attempting to change that data. Note that a file *must* be used exclusively (see below) before the PACK, REINDEX, or ZAP commands can be issued.

On Record Sharing

Once you have decided that it is alright to share a database file, you must then choose whether to share or lock individual records. When a record is locked, only the locking user can update the information in that record. As with files, you must lock individual records only when a user is going to write data for those records to a database file with commands such as @...SAY...GET, DELETE, RECALL, or REPLACE.

Data Update Visibility

Since a networking environment is made up of many users and processes, a network application programmer must be aware of when data updates become available, or *visible*, to those other processes. This is especially important because a network may not actually write data to disk until a specific command is given; if the system crashes before that command is issued, the data could be lost.

Although visibility can be a complex issue, you will be safe if you follow these general rules: Using UNLOCK on a file or record will guarantee that other users (or other processes) can then see the current user's changes; safer still is closing the file or performing a COMMIT. These commands force the data to be written to disk, thus allowing all other users to see the new data, and also ensuring the integrity of the new data.

NETWORK PROGRAMMING COMMANDS

Now that the ideas behind network programming have been introduced, it is time to get down to the details. In all, you will need only six commands and functions for most of your Clipper networking tasks. Because the uses of these commands are so interwoven, examples will be given at the end of this discussion.

Selecting the Networking Mode

Networking with the USE command

Whenever you open a file, you can decide whether it can be shared or used exclusively by a single user. You make this decision with an option of the USE command (see Step 13). The syntax for this command is:

```
USE ... [ EXCLUSIVE | SHARED ]
```

Although the default is EXCLUSIVE, every USE command in an application employed in a network environment should explicitly specify the networking mode. Here is an example:

```
USE Cust EXCLUSIVE
```

Because a USE like this one could fail (if the file were already locked by another user), you should not specify indexes with the INDEX clause of the USE command. Instead, you should use SET INDEX (see the example below).

Network Error Checking

Because failure to achieve a file or record lock is a common occurrence in a network, a function is provided that reports whether or not the most recent network file operation has succeeded. It is NETERR(). It returns a true value (.T.) if the most recent USE or APPEND BLANK has failed.

Locking Files

FLOCK()

The Clipper function FLOCK() attempts to lock the current database file. If it is successful, it returns a true (.T.); otherwise, it returns a false (.F.). Any attempted FLOCK() unlocks any record or file previously locked by the current user.

Locking Records

RLOCK()

The Clipper function RLOCK() attempts to lock the current record. Like FLOCK(), if successful it returns a true (.T.); otherwise, it returns a false (.F.). Any attempted RLOCK() also unlocks any record or file previously locked by the current user.

Releasing File or Record Locks

UNLOCK()

To release the file or record lock on the current database file, use the Clipper command UNLOCK. The command

```
UNLOCK ALL
```

releases every lock set in every work area.

Forcing a Disk Write

COMMIT

As discussed above, a network will not necessarily write your data to disk just because you removed the current record or file lock. To ensure the disk write, you could close the database file, but that might be inconvenient. Clipper provides another command that forces a disk write: COMMIT. For example, you could change the relevant section in ADD.PRG to:

```
REPLACE Custnum WITH aCust, Lastname WITH ;
  aLast, Firstname WITH aFirst, Address WITH ;
```

```
    aAdd, City WITH aCity, State WITH aState, ;
    Zip WITH aZip
  COMMIT
```

NETWORK PROGRAMMING EXAMPLE

Whenever you attempt to open or lock a file (or record) in a network environment with the above commands, you must be prepared to deal with failure. Not only might another user be using (or locking) the desired data, but the network might be busy with another task that does not allow the immediate satisfaction of the open or lock request. Thus, you must write your code to deal with the possibility of file-locking or opening failure.

Dealing with File-Locking or Opening Failure

When writing code to deal with locking or opening failures on a network, you generally do two things: create a system for retrying the request a fixed number of times or seconds; and provide the user with information about the status of the request, including the possibility of aborting or retrying the file lock or open request.

File Locking Example

Here is a function that tries to execute a file lock. The argument specifies the amount of time (in seconds) during which *LockFile()* tries to obtain the lock. Each attempt lasts one second.

```
FUNCTION LockFile( tTime )
LOCAL Elapsed := 0
IF FLOCK()
  RETURN  .T. // File successfully locked.
ENDIF
DO WHILE Elapsed < tTime
  INKEY(1) // Wait one second.
  Elapsed := Elapsed + 1 // Increment counter
```

```
    IF FLOCK()
      RETURN  .T. // File lock achieved.
    ENDIF
  ENDDO
  RETURN (.F.) // Lock attempt failed.
```

You could use this function, for example, in a network application in which you wanted to delete multiple records from a database. The next example is a code fragment demonstrating *LockFile()*. It includes a five-second attempt to lock the file.

The DO WHILE loop repeats until a lock is obtained or the user decides to quit trying.

File locking with user partici-pation

```
lScreen := SAVESCREEN( 0, 0, MAXROW(), ;
  MAXCOL() )
DO WHILE !LockFile( 5 )
  // Repeat while lock fails.
  @ 12, 5 CLEAR TO 18, 30
  @ 12, 5 TO 18, 30 DOUBLE
  @ 14, 6 SAY PADC(  "File Lock Failed ", 24 )
  @ 16, 10 SAY  "Retry (Y/N)? "
  @ 16, 23 GET Retry_It PICTURE  "Y "
  READ
  IF Retry_It // Reattempt the lock.
    LOOP
  ELSE // Return to the calling procedure.
    CLEAR // Clean up the screen.
    RESTSCREEN( lScreen )
    USE // Close the active work area.
    RETURN // Quit the procedure.
  ENDIF
ENDDO
RESTSCREEN( lScreen )
/*  Continue deletion code here after
successful lock.  */
```

Of course, this code is just an example; it would have to be modified to fit into your software. A function similar to *LockFile()* could be used for testing record locking.

File Opening Example

Another common networking operation is a file open. Any time you open a database file, there is the possibility of failure, either because of network errors or a previous lock on that file by another user. Here is a simple example of such an operation. Greater user involvement and repeated file open requests (as in the example above) could, of course, be added.

```
USE Cust SHARED
IF NETERR() // Returns .T. if the USE failed.
  @ 10, 15 SAY ;
    "The desired file is currently unavailable. "
  INKEY(5) /* Give the user 5 seconds to read
    the message.*/
  RETURN /* Exit the current procedure on
    failure.*/
ELSE
  SET INDEX TO Custnum // Setup the index file.
ENDIF
```

A Few Final Considerations

Printing on networks

Remember to execute the COMMIT command after a file write operation to ensure the integrity of your data. While you can use the SET PRINTER TO command (see Step 17) to select among multiple printers on a network, you will probably want to use the network to establish which printer will be used. Printing on networks can be tricky; make sure that you follow the directions in your network documentation exactly to get the output you desire. Also make sure to test your software fully in multiuser mode before delivering it to your client.

BEYOND THIS STEP

Network programming is always more difficult than it sounds. Make sure your software is thoroughly tested in multiuser mode before delivering it to your client. Check every file-related Clipper command to make sure that it functions correctly in your network environment.

D

E

F

G

M

N

O

S

T

U

V

W

X

Y

Z

Selections from The SYBEX Library

DATABASES

The ABC's of dBASE III PLUS
Robert Cowart
264pp. Ref. 379-1
The most efficient way to get beginners up and running with dBASE. Every 'how' and 'why' of database management is demonstrated through tutorials and practical dBASE III PLUS applications.

The ABC's of dBASE IV 1.1
Robert Cowart
350pp, Ref. 632-4
The latest version of dBASE IV is featured in this hands-on introduction. It assumes no previous experience with computers or database management, and uses easy-to-follow lessons to introduce the concepts, build basic skills, and set up some practical applications. Includes report writing and Query by Example.

The ABC's of Paradox 3.5 (Second Edition)
Charles Siegel
334pp, Ref. 785-1
This easy-to-follow, hands-on tutorial is a must for beginning users of Paradox 3.0 and 3.5. Even if you've never used a computer before, you'll be doing useful work in just a few short lessons. A clear introduction to database management and valuable business examples make this a "right-to-work" guide for the practical-minded.

Advanced Techniques in dBASE III PLUS
Alan Simpson
454pp. Ref. 369-4
A full course in database design and structured programming, with routines for inventory control, accounts receivable, system management, and integrated databases.

dBASE Instant Reference SYBEX Prompter Series
Alan Simpson
471pp. Ref. 484-4; 4 3/4" × 8"
Comprehensive information at a glance: a brief explanation of syntax and usage for every dBASE command, with step-by-step instructions and exact keystroke sequences. Commands are grouped by function in twenty precise categories.

dBASE III PLUS Programmer's Reference Guide SYBEX Ready Reference Series
Alan Simpson
1056pp. Ref. 508-5
Programmers will save untold hours and effort using this comprehensive, well-organized dBASE encyclopedia. Complete technical details on commands and functions, plus scores of often-needed algorithms.

dBASE IV 1.1 Programmer's Instant Reference (Second Edition)
Alan Simpson
555pp, Ref. 764-9
Enjoy fast, easy access to information often hidden in cumbersome documentation. This handy pocket-sized reference presents information on each command and function in the dBASE IV programming language. Commands are grouped according to their purpose, so readers can locate the correct command for any task—quickly and easily.

dBASE IV User's Instant Reference (Second Edition)
Alan Simpson
356pp, Ref. 786-X
Completely revised to cover the new 1.1 version of dBASE IV, this handy reference guide presents information on every dBASE operation a user can perform. Exact keystroke sequences are presented, and complex tasks are explained step-by-step. It's a great way for newer users to look up the basics, while more experienced users will find it a fast way to locate information on specialized tasks.

Mastering dBASE III PLUS: A Structured Approach
Carl Townsend
342pp. Ref. 372-4
In-depth treatment of structured programming for custom dBASE solutions. An ideal study and reference guide for applications

developers, new and experienced users with an interest in efficient programming.

Mastering dBASE IV Programming

Carl Townsend

496pp. Ref. 540-9

This task-oriented book introduces structured dBASE IV programming and commands by setting up a general ledger system, an invoice system, and a quotation management system. The author carefully explores the unique character of dBASE IV based on his in-depth understanding of the program.

Mastering FoxPro

Charles Seigel

639pp. Ref. 671-5

This guide to the powerful FoxPro DBMS offers a tutorial on database basics, then enables the reader to master new skills and features as needed—with many examples from business. An in-depth tutorial guides users through the development of a complete mailing list system.

Mastering Paradox 3.5

Alan Simpson

650pp, Ref. 677-4

This indispensable, in-depth guide has again been updated for the latest Paradox release, offering the same comprehensive, hands-on treatment featured in highly praised previous editions. It covers everything from database basics to PAL programming—including complex queries and reports, and multi-table applications.

Mastering Q & A (Second Edition)

Greg Harvey

540pp. Ref. 452-6

This hands-on tutorial explores the Q & A Write, File, and Report modules, and the Intelligent Assistant. English-language command processor, macro creation, interfacing with other software, and more, using practical business examples.

Power User's Guide to R:BASE

Alan Simpson
Cheryl Currid
Craig Gillett

446pp. Ref. 354-6

Supercharge your R:BASE applications with this straightforward tutorial that covers system design, structured programming, managing multiple data tables, and more. Sample applications include ready-to-run mailing, inventory and accounts receivable systems. Through Version 2.11.

Understanding dBASE III

Alan Simpson

300pp. Ref. 267-1

dBASE commands and concepts are illustrated throughout with practical, business oriented examples—for mailing list handling, accounts receivable, and inventory design. Contains scores of tips and techniques for maximizing efficiency and meeting special needs.

Understanding dBASE III PLUS

Alan Simpson

415pp. Ref. 349-X

A solid sourcebook of training and ongoing support. Everything from creating a first database to command file programming is presented in working examples, with tips and techniques you won't find anywhere else.

Understanding dBASE IV 1.1

Alan Simpson

900pp, Ref. 633-2

Simpson's outstanding introduction to dBASE—brought up to date for version 1.1—uses tutorials and practical examples to build effective, and increasingly sophisticated, database management skills. Advanced topics include custom reporting, managing multiple databases, and designing custom applications.

Understanding Oracle

James T. Perry
Joseph G. Lateer

634pp. Ref. 534-4

A comprehensive guide to the Oracle database management system for administrators, users, and applications developers. Covers everything in Version 5 from database basics to multi-user systems, performance, and development tools including SQL*Forms, SQL*Report, and SQL*Calc. Includes Fast Track speed notes.

Clipper Quick Reference Guide
continued

DBU: DATABASE UTILITY MENU CHOICES

F1	Help	
F2	Open	Database; Index; View
F3	Create	Database; Index
F4	Save	View; Struct
F5	Browse	Database; View
F6	Utility	Copy; Append; Replace; Pack Zap; Run
F7	Move	Seek; Goto; Locate; Skip
F8	Set	Relation; Filter; Fields

CLD: CLIPPER DEBUGGER FUNCTION KEYS

F1	Help	Displays information about CLD
F2	Zoom	Toggles the size of the Watch or Callstack windows
F3	Retype Last Command	Retypes the last command entered in the Command window
F4	Application Screen	Displays current program screen output
F5	Execute Application	Runs program until breakpoint or tracepoint, or until Alt-D is pressed
F6	Show Status	Displays the database information window